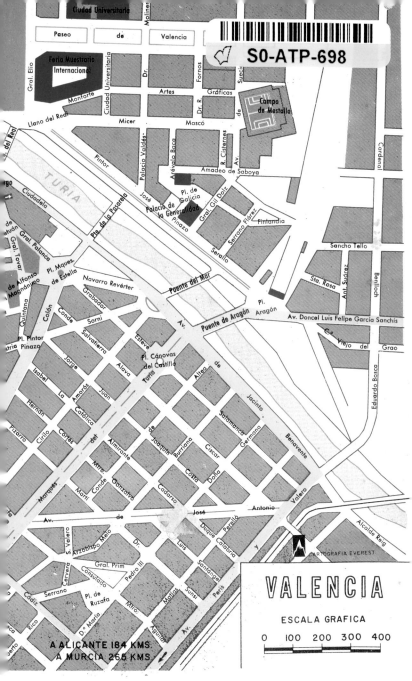

S0-ATP-698

VALENCIA

ESCALA GRAFICA

0   100 200 300 400

A ALICANTE 184 KMS.
A MURCIA 265 KMS.

VALENCIA

TERCERA EDICION

Texts: Francisco Almela y Vives.

Photographs: Valentín Pla.
A. Mas.
Oronoz.

Archivo gráfico del Ministerio de Información y Turismo.

EDITORIAL EV~~ERE~~ST

Apartado 339 - LEÓN (España)

A CITY, IN ITS LIGHT

The city of Valencia —as we well know— is situated on the shores of the Mediterranean, approximately in the middle of the gulf os the same name. Its climate is temperate; summers with sea breezes and winters with brilliant sunshine. The population, according to the latest official statistics, amounts to 584,672 inhabitants.

But there is nothing less exact than numbers... And in large amounts everything is relative... This is especially so in the case of this city, as Valencia is surrounded by suburbs, towns and even cities, sometimes without any separations. Every morning the city is fraternally «invaded» by thousands who come to work, for business purposes or pleasure and stay there until the evening, when they «abandon» same to return to their respective homes.

Those thousands and thousands of people who come by train, bus or car, give the city a certain feeling of being alive, which is one of its particular characteristics. Some foreing writer has also observed that the majority of people to be found in the streets and squares, wear expressions of calm, of euphoria, so different from the serious expressions, when they are not gloomy, which are so prevalent in many parts of the world.

Another characteristic of Valencia is its light, which is with reason called «La Clara».

With regard to the rest, this is a population which cannot be defined with just one word. Because, even though it is old, with its secular monuments and traditional customs, it is also new, with complete, newly built districts. Because, even though it is an agricultural centre (oranges, rice, etc.), it also has maritime interests (the port, beaches) and an industrial centre (furniture, metals). Because, even though it is a working city, the population also knows how to enjoy themselves...

Is there a lack of personality? No, because the personality maybe consists of those —and other— dualities. All this is apart from the fact that everything —both material and spiritual— seems and almost appears to be united by the light. A French Hispanist, Maurice Legendre, wrote: «This light, which is so sheer in its intensity, is the one which gives an original character to the products of Valencia, and above all to the spritis».

The Avenida de Jose Antonio. →

Partial view of Valencia.

The Avenida de Fernando el Catolico.

Another partial view of the beautiful Valencian capital.

SOME HISTORICAL INFORMATION

Apart from the antecedents which have been given and can still be given by Prehistory, Protohistory and Archeology, we can still state that the city of Valencia, which was founded in the year 138 B.C., according to popular opinion, is more than two thousand years old.

From the start of the Christian era, the population —with its status as a Roman colony, and benefit of the Itallic Law— lived a normal life, if we can call it such. Then in the year 304, Publius Dacianus, who was an enemy of Christianity, arrested Valero, Bishop of Zaragoza, together with his Deacon, Vicente. He had them transferred to the Ciudad del Turia, where they were martyred. That is why St. Vicent, the Martyr, is the patron saint of the city.

During the Visigoth period, Valencia stands out several times, as for example when Leovigildo exiled his son Hermenegildo there. When the Arab invasion took place, Tarik took possession of the city, which became successively head of «waliato» and of an emir, and assimilated the Muslem culture of which there were distinguished followers.

After an ephimeral rule by El Cid, enhanced by Literature, Valencia returned to Muslem rule, until 1238 when King Jaime II of Aragon conquered it definitely for western civilization, establishing it as the head of a Kingdom with its own laws, which existed for more than four and a half centuries. The 15th century in Valencia was singularly splendid in the literary, artistic, economic, urban, etc. aspects.

At the beginning of the 18th Century, the City and the Kingdom of Valencia took part in the War of Succession in favour of Archduke Charles of Austria, therefore, Philip V, as victor, abolished Valencia's privileges. However, when the city was able to recover from the war, the city experienced a period of prosperity, thanks for the most part to the importance given at that time to the silk industry.

At the beginning of the 19th century, Valencia actively took part in the struggle against Napoleon and then had to relfect, in the same way, the general events in Spain, at the same time as it increased in importance, which was helped by the wealth obtained from the export of agricultural products.

With the Regional and National Exhibitions in 1909 and 1910, the City of Valencia began the modern era.

Monument to the Conqueror of Valencia, Jaime I of Aragon.

Municipal Historical Museum: The «Senyera» and the «Taula de Canvis».

Codex of the «Consolat del Mar». Shield of Valencia, in the Fine Arts Museum.

«I shall stay in Valencia. Valencia is my property».

View of the Turia, with the Serranos bridge.

Small altar on the Puente del Real.

THE RIVER TURIA

The source of the River Turia is to be found in some springs in the Municipal terminus of Guadalviar, in the Burrough of Albarracin in the province of Teruel. After a rugged course, it comes to the plains, with a 296 kilometer stretch, until it flows gently into the Mediterranean.

During its course, the river has been bled by the irrigation ditches of Real de Moncada, Quarte, Tormos, Mislata, Mestalla, Fabra, Rascanya, Rovella, and finally the Acequia de Oro. The representatives of the seven contained between the first and the last of the ones listed above, form the very ancient Water Tribune, which meets every Thursday at mid-day outside the Cathedral door of the Apostles, to punish the infractions of the irrigators and to settle the disputes among them. Everything is done verbally, without any paperwork, and quickly.

The River Turia, for many centuries, has formed on its way through the City of Valencia a smooth arch between the city shell and several suburbs. For intercommunication between the former and the latter, the bridges of San Jose, Serranos, Trinidad, Real and Mar, between ogival and baroque, as they have had to be reconstructed on occasions, were built. Some of these bridges —of beautiful architecture— display characteristic temples with sculptured images. Kilometers of brick walls on both sides of the river form a unique example, which in times past were carried out by two municipal organizations, called Fabrica Vella dita de Murs i Valls (Old Masonry of Walls and Fences) and Fabrica Nova dita del Riu (New Masonry of the River), with taxes on corn and meat respectively.

This river course was in a certain way progenitor of the city which with reason is known as the Ciudad del Turia, as in remote times the contributions of those waters formed the land on which the city was built. It was also to help to maintain the city, when the latter was directly or indirectly of an agricultural nature. But at the sametime it was to cause the city a great deal of havoc with repeated floods, such as the one in 1957. Since then, from among the various solutions for avoiding the dangers of the floods, it has been decided to branch off the river, which is being done at the moment.

The thousand year old Water Tribune.

Water Tribune bailiff._

THE TESTIMONIES OF THE WALLS

Until 1356 the city of Valencia had some more or less efficient walls, which were then considered void or insufficient. Remains of those walls, built of mortar, can be seen or found absorbed in a certain part of the Carmen district, which can be centred on the picturesque and evoking Portal de Valldigna, which formed part of the said walls. There is, very close to this door, a turret which was declared a historic-artistic monument in 1963, and which cannot be seen from the street, but only from the back part of some buildings. Not far from there, in the part known as El Tossal, is the postern of the Caldereria, although provisionally hidden, belonging to the same defense system.

However, in the said year of 1356, the Council of the City, with the approval of Pedro the Ceremonious, agreed to construct new walls, which were in fact built and stood until the second half of the 19th century. In 1865, they were all raised to the ground, including some doors which were real monuments of an artistic nature. Only the doors of the Serranos and Quart were saved, because the towers of both were used as prisons.

The door of the Serranos was completely built of stone between 1393 and 1398, by the stonemason Pere Balaguer, with various collaborators. Apart from his salary, the rent of his house was also paid for... so that he could be closer to the work. This gate is inspired in the Puerta Real of the Poblet monastery, although it exceeds the latter in slimness and ornamental beauty and presents technical peculiarities such as being open in the cyma. The whole set up resembles a triumphal arch rather than a defense construction. And it served as such on many occasions.

With regard to the Quart door, it was constructed between 1441 and 1460 by Pere Bonfill, probably inspired by the Castel Nuovo in Naples, but without architectonic refinement. However, the bulk and height of the flanking towers, which are of stone and mortar, are impressive. Shell marks in the towers remind us that they played an important part in the wars against invaders and in domestic struggles.

— Valldigna Portal in the El Carmen District.

Gateway and Serranos Towers.

Cuarte or Quart Towers. →

Town Hall Façade.

«Cañas y barros» (Canes and clay). ➞

Panoramic view of Valencia.

THE CITY'S HOUSE

The Jurors and Councillors to whom Don Jaime the Conqueror entrusted the government of the city of Valencia, did not take long to decide that their primitive abode was insufficient. In 1311, Don Jaime II authorized them to acquire some sites —at the beginning of what is today the Calle de los Caballeros— where they built the City's House. With the times, the latter has undergone several changes and has been enriched with works of art and craft. In about the middle of the 19th century, as the building was beginning to show signs of age, it was decided not to reinforce it but to pull it down —not without controversy— and this was done between 1854 and 1860.

Then, with the permission of the Civil Governor, the Town Hall was installed in the saw called Casa Enseñanza (Teaching House), built in the middle of the 18th century by the Archbishop of Valencia, Andres Mayoral, for the instruction and education of girls. It was a building of severe architectural design, even more accentuated by the great iron bars of which there were many.

At the beginning of this century, some buildings which had first been the convent of St. Francis and then barracks, were demolished leaving free some sites —today the Plaza del Caudillo— which were used for building a new façade which was to be joined on to the old building. The first stone of this façade —the work of the architects Carlos Carbonell and Francisco Mora— was placed in 1906 but the work was not finished until the twenties. The said façade has a tower at each end, with stilted cupolas, and a central body topped by the clock tower. The sculptured decoration consists of four statues depicting Prudence, Strength, Temperance and Justice, worked by Carmelo Vicent who did the two side ones and by Vicente Beltrán who did the two central ones. Mariano Benlliure was responsible for the two nude women in the pendentives and a shield of Valencia with two nude women supporting the latter.

The points worthy of note in the City's House are the Session Hall and the Ballroom, with paintings and sculptures by modern Valencian artists, as well as the Historical Museum, which is dealt with in more detail further on in this book.

▸— Botanical Garden.

Town Hall. The Sala Foral.

The Ballroom. ⟶

THE PALACE OF THE «GENERALIDAD»

The Deputation of the «Generalidad» of the Kingdom of Valencia —called in short La Generalitat, in the language of the country— was created as a permanent representation of the Parliament for collecting a so called «general» tax, as it affected everyone, including the king; it was formally constituted in the Monzon Parliaments (1417) and over the course of time it was increased in the number of components and functions.

The increase of the institution led to the obtention of buildings between 1422 and 1482 which were demolished and the sites used for the construction of the Palace of the «Generalidad».

The «mason» Francesc Martinez de Viulaygua and the stone masons Joan Guiverro and Pere Compte displayed their skills in the construction of the main body of the building.

Later on (1618-1685) a large turret, planned by the master Montano and executed not without difficulties, was built next to the afore-mentioned body of the building. The slowness of the construction is revealed in the diversity of styles, which go from Gothic to Herrerian, passing through renaissance, without this damaging the aesthetics of the whole.

However, the greatest beauty of the turret is to be found in its contents, and above all in the marvellous caissoned ceilings of the mezzanine, mainly the work of the carpinter Genis Linares, continued by his son Pere. What virtuosity in the carving of the caissons! What extravagance in the application of gold! What elegance in the touches of colour! Linares also worked on the caissoned ceiling in the great hall on the main floor, the galleries of which were carved by the carpenter Gaspar Gregori, which is all in the natural colour of the wood. This hall, which is incorrectly called the Parliament hall, as the latter never met here, has its walls covered with canvases by Juan Saranyena (or Sariñena) and others (18th century) which represent a session of the Deputation of the «Generalidad» and several estates from which the deputies came.

When Valencia's privileges were abolished in 1707, it was not long before the institution in question disappeared and the palace was occupied by the Courts until 1922. The Provincial Deputation then took over the building, cleaned it up and carried out the old project, which consisted of another turret exactly the same as the first one.

Palace of the «Generalidad». ➞

Palace of the «Generalidad» - Courtyard.

Caissoned ceiling in the Gold room.

THE UNIVERSITY

Putting aside all antecedents, it is positive that the University of Valencia was founded, for clearly municipal purposes, by means of a bull issued by Pope Alexander VI in 1501 and a privilege granted by Ferdinand, the Catholic King, in 1502. The institution was installed in a building previously constructed by the already men-. tioned stonemason Compte and the mason Benia. During its existence, it has undergone natural vicissitudes, although as a whole it has had a good set of professors and students.

The present building which in general dates from 1830, is of a severe neo-classical design, both outside and in the courtyard with double doric columns, the upper one built in modern times. This building absorbed the Assembly Hall, which was designed by the distinguished mathemetician, P. Tomas Vicente Tosca in the first third of the 18th century; this hall displays an insteresting gallery of potraits of distinguished people connected with the University. This building also preserves the chapel, also of the 18th century, with a Gothic panel representing the Virgin of Wisdom.

The University and Provincial Library is very valuable, not only on account of the amount of its funds, but also on account of the quality of same. Special mention should be made of the very rich collection of codexes of the Duke of Calabria, who was viceroy of Valencia. Among the incunabuli there are such extraordinary pieces as the Trobes de la Verge María (unique copy), which is considered as the first book to be printed in Spain, and the first edition of Tirant lo Blanc, the novel of chivalry praised by Cervantes.

An architectonic fountain, attached to one of the façades of this building, was inaugurated in 1966, with sculptures by Octavio Vicent, representing the Rector Vicente Blasco, who reorganized the University at the end of the 18th century, Alexander VI, Valencia (an allegorical female figure), Ferdinand, the Catholic King, and his wife.

The Science, Medicine and Law faculties are installed on the Paseo al Mar, as well as the Agricultural Engineers College and other teaching establishments. The Arts Faculty is also being built there. The old university building will be used as the rectorate, general library, etc., with the statue of Juan Luis Vives, by Jose Aixa in 1880, in the centre of the courtyard.

◄— Palace of the «Generalidad». Caissoned ceiling and gallery
of the room called the Parliament hall.

The University courtyard, with the monument to Juan Luis Vives.

University. Speech Room.

An illustration from the manuscript of the «Roman de la Rose»
in the University library.

The modern Law Faculty.

Fountain in a corner of the University.

THE PALACE OF JUSTICE

The Parliament of the Kingdom of Valencia, held in 1626, in accordance with the wishes of the King. Philip IV of Castile, had to establish the tax known as «revised entrance rights». In order to regulate the complicated exaction of same, several chapters were agreed, including one which covered the building of a customs office.

This collecting office had three more or less provisional buildings. But the intendent, Jose Aviles, presented King Ferdinand VI with the plans for a new building for the Customs Office. Work began in 1758 and was paid for from the taxes collected off the people of Valencia on all edible goods which came into the town. The work was directed by Felipe Rubio, mason and Tomas Miner, stonemason. In anyway, it is said that the former was helped by his brother-in-law, Antonio Gilbert, an architect, whose intervention was especially contracted for the main door and the staircase.

The finished building was trully magnificent for those times and continues to be one of the City's most important buildings to this day. It forms a complete, rectangular shaped block. The façades are decorated with doric pilasters. On the cornice there is a beautiful balustrade, on which the banisters in groups of four alternate with dormer windows or skylights, effective or decorative, and stone pommels or pinnacles. The main façade is marked with a half circle arch, under which there is a balcony, followed by a large shield in relief of the monarch referred to in the inscription: «Don Carlos III. Año 1760». This date is taken as the one marking the end of the work.

Topping this façade there is a statue of the monarch Charles III, flanked on both sides by two reclining matrons, representing Justice and Prudence. The whole ensemble is a very notable work by Ignacio Vergara, who also did the shield.

The interior of the building —in which the monumental staircase should be noted— has undergone many changes, in view of the various uses to which it has been destined. At first it housed, apart from the Customs Office, other public offices. Between 1828 and well into the present century, it was a tobacco factory and in 1922 it was inagurated as the Palace of Justice.

Three views of the Palace of Justice, built to house the Customs
in the 18th century.

THE MERCHANTS' EXCHANGE

The Merchants' Exchange —also known as the Seda (Silk), because at one time it was mainly used for the transaction of this product— is the most beautiful Gothic monument, of a civil nature, in Valencia, and one of the best in Spain.

As the original Exchange was inadequate, the present one was built between 1482 and 1498 on the initiative and at the expense of the city Council. The principal figure who intervened in the construction of same was the already mentioned Pere Compte, who was simply entitled a stonemason, although he carried out the difficult tasks of architect and engineer.

The monument —which occupies an approximately rectangular area of 1,990 square meters— consists of three main building bodies and a garden. The main body contains the large contracting hall with helicoidal columns, which open up into palms to form the ribbing of the vault, reminding us of ropes for mooring boats or skeins of silk. Next to this impressive hall, there is a turret, with a staircase of 110 steps without a central shaft, which is a real technical feat. This turret joins up with the third body of the building or Consulate pavilion, where the said institution met. The outside, in the top part, is of a beautiful renaissance nature. Inside, there is a very valuable ceiling from the former, demolished City's House. With regard to the architectonic elegance of the monument, it is completed with an extraordinary sculptured decoration; gargoyles, shields, realistic or imaginative reliefs...

The Exchange, as has been already stated, was built for merchanting purposes, and, therefore, there is a frieze in the main room recommending the merchants not to cheat, not to swear under false pretences or to lend money on interest. But it was also used for other purposes and, at present, apart from housing the new Exchange Consulate, it is also the headquarters for the Centre of Valencian Culture.

A distinguished man from Segovia, the Marquis of Lozoya, an art historian, stated that the Valencia Exchange «is one of the top monuments of Hispanic art» and that «even in the richest cities in France, Flanders or Italy, nothing similar was done for the service of commerce».

Main façade of the Exchange. ⟶

Exchange. Entrance door to the Valencian Cultural Centre.

Exchange. Two sculptured details.

Exchange. The great Contracting Hall.

Exchange. Courtyard and garden, formerly known as the Orange Garden.

Detail of the Cathedral's Apostles door and façade
of the Basilica of the Virgin of the Helpless.   →

THE CATHEDRAL

Valencia's Cathedral occupies, at least in part, the site of the high mosque. King James I of Aragon ordered the Arab temple to be consecrated and to be provisionally destined as a Christian church. The first stone for the final church was placed in 1262. It can be considered that the church was finished in 1356 or 1376, although the name of the architect who planned, directed or executed the work, in Gothic style, is unknown. The church underwent several reforms or enlargements, until in the 18th century, the architects Antonio Gilabert and Lorenzo Martinez carried out a much disputed rennovation in a neoclassical style, which affected almost the whole of the interior of the building.

The variety of style of the Seo Valentina is shown in the three doors as seen from the outside. The main part of the Palau door, in the Plaza de la Almoina, is Romanic and the rest Gothic, although a Mudejar influence is also evident, forming an interesting ensemble. The Apostles door, in the Plaza de la Virgen, is ogival, with numerous sculptures and topped by an elegant tracery opening, called Salomó, as it contains the sign of Solomon (two equilateral triangles combined to form a six pointed star). Finally, the main door, popularly known as the Iron Door on account of the artistic grille, is a magnificent baroque work, conceived and partly executed by the German architect, Conrad Rodulfo, in concave form, who had to flee during the War of Succession. His work, mainly the sculptured part, was continued by Ignacio Vergara and others.

Inside the church, we should point out numerous pictures, sculptures, and tombs, such as that of the great poet Ausias March, indicated by a modern tombstone. The Baroque presbytery preserves the double doors used for covering a large silver altarpiece, which has since disappeared; the doors are formed out of twelve canvases by Hernando Yáñez de la Almedina and Hernando Llanos, a very valuable Renaissance production, which led one monarch to declare that if the altarpiece was of silver, the doors were of gold.

One of the reforms carried out since 1939, consists in the construction of a marble ciborium —work of the architect Vicente Traver— in the centre of the transept, exactly under the dome or lantern of the 14th century, one of the main architectonic splendours of the Cathedral, which —according to the treatise writer Lamperez and Romea— «is of an imponderable translucency and beauty».

Cathedral. Main façade (18th century). ⟶

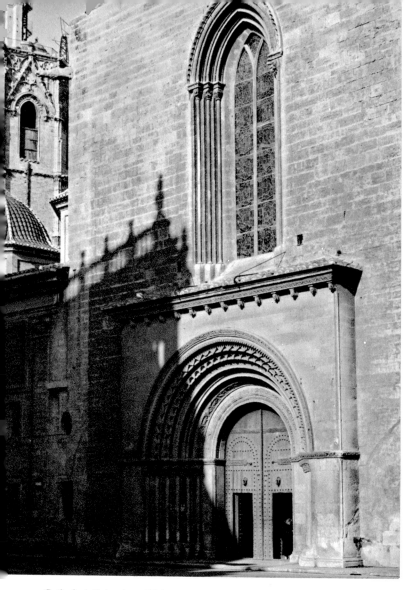

Cathedral. Palau door (13th century).

Apostles Door. ⟶

Cathedral. Dome.

Interior of the Cathedral.

Detail of the Adoration of the Shepherds by Yañez de la Almedina.

THE CHALICE OF THE LAST SUPPER

One of the most highly suggestive parts of the Cathedral is the today so-called Chapel of the Holy Chalice, built in the middle of the 14th century, by an unknown master, as a capitular and study room. In the 18th century an architectonic Gothic style ensemble was applied to the apse from the transept of the church itself; recently twelve alabaster marble reliefs were added to this ensemble of scenes from the Old and New Testament, worked by Juliano Florentino, a disciple of Ghiberti; these reliefs are considered as «the best Florentine Renaissance work outside Florence». Furthermore, in the centre of the thus described altarpiece is a hollow in which the Chalice of the Last Supper is placed.

The Gospels recount that on the Feast of the Pass Over, Jesus foregathered with his disciples in the house of a noble well-to-do man. Under the general name of Supper, he held several acts there, including the institution of the Eucharist. Among the various glasses used figured the one used in this most important institution, on account of which it could not be forgotten.

This explains why it appeared later in Rome, probably taken by St. Peter. After about two and a half centuries, Emperor Valerius unleashed a persecution against Christianism, in which the Pope, Sixtus II, perished; but the latter, before dying a martyr, gave the Holy Chalice to his deacon Lorenzo, who was from Huesca, and who in turn sent the goblet to Huesca (in 258 or 261), together with a letter.

At the time of the Muslem invasion, Audeberto, the Bishop of Huesca, took refuge with the Chalice in the spot on which the Monastery of San Juan de la Peña was to be founded; and according to testified decree, this famous relic was kept here until 1134. Martin el Humano managed to persuade the monks of that monastery to give him the Chalice, according to a document, in 1399. During the reign of Alfonso the Magnanimous it went from the Aljaferia in Zaragoza to the Royal Treasury in Valencia. This monarch's lieutenant ordered the Holy Goblet to be transferred for better keeping to the Cathedral.

A Catalan specialist, Dr. Trens, has said: «Archeology is in favour of the antiquity of the goblet, and the History of Art cannot but considerer its mounting as a piece of exceptional value, which only a very ancient and deep rooted devotion towards this relic can explain».

Cathedral. The Holy Chalice.

Alabaster reliefs by Juliano Florentino, in the chapel
of the Holy Chalice.

Girls dressed in the traditional costume.

THE «MICALET»

On the initiative of the bishop of Valencia, Don Jaime de Aragon, a first cousin to the king Peter the Ceremonious, the construction of a new bell tower was begun in 1381 in accordance with the Council of the Seo Valentina.

The first architect was Andreu Juliá, who made his work on this tower compatible with the work he was doing in Tortosa, travelling from one city to the other on hired mules. For the rest, his studio —to call it something— was a cane shed; his board a flower bed in the Ruzafa orchard; his instruments, some string, nails and planks; his couch, a mountain of straw... He was succeded by Joseph Franch, who went to Lerida to look at the bell tower of the Cathedral three. Another of the architects was Pere Balaguer, whose trip was paid to Narbona and other towns to see bell towers. This made the English architect and writer, George Edmund Street (19th century) say: «I know of few events in the history of the world which are of more interest than the accounts made of this case». Pere Balaguer was probably the author of the fourth body, which is beautifull decorated, of this tower. Marti Llobet finished it off with an openwork parapet and other elements which had to be taken down in the 18th century on account of deterioration.

The said belfry is 51 meters high, the same as its perimeter. Its form is that of an octagonal prism, the sides of which are divided with moldings, in the same way as the four sections making up the tower. The construction is a solid as can be with a 207 step staircase, two small rooms and another room —in the fourth section of the tower— where eleven bells are housed. Apart from these eleven bells, there are two more bells on the terrace for sounding the hour and the quarters. The first of these substitutes others, weighs almost 11,000 kgs., and, in the same way as its predecessors, is called Miguel, or more exactly, Miquel, the diminutives being Miguelete and Micalet respectively.

The latter name is the one which is given, with affection and because of metonymy, to the distinguished, extremely strong tower, which is so deeply involved in so many aspects of life in Valencia. It is, therefore, with reason, that this tower is a symbol for all the people of Valencia and especially for all those who are a long way from the city.

◄— El Micalet, the Cathedral Tower.

◄— Fans: a craft which still persists.

← Partial view of the Micalet.

Corpus Christi or Patriarch college.

THE COLLEGE OF THE PATRIARCH

This simple expression is the one used among the people of Valencia for naming a foundation of San Juan de Ribera, who apart from being Patriarch of Antioch, was Archbishop, Vice-roy and general Captain of Valencia and chancellor of its University. The purpose of the foundation, instituted in 1583, was to better the traditional High Schools and to guide them in the best method of obtaining the goals proposed by the Council of Trent with the establishment of Seminaries. The Patriarch drew up detailed Constitutions for this foundation which have been observed both internally as well as in acts of worship, which are unequalled in solemnity.

The first stone of the College-Seminary and attached church —or Chapel— was placed on 30th October 1586. The Chapel, although the College had not yet been finished, was inaugurated on 8th February 1604, taking advantage of the fact that Philip III was in Valencia.

The technical direction of the architectonic part seems to have been carried out by Guillem del Rey. We should also add that numerous stonemasons, painters, cabinetmakers, bronzesmiths, ceramists, etc. worked on the construction and decoration.

The church is of severe correct lines, with abundant pictorical decoration, by Bartolome Matarana and others. The body of the founder, who died in 1611, is buried in one of the chapels. From among the church's paintings we pick out the «Last Supper», a masterpiece by Francisco Ribalta, in the presbytery.

Guillem del Rey, mentioned above, took advantage of some Genoese marmoreal columns and constructed «the most beautiful Spanish Renaissance cloister». In the centre of this cloister there is a sitting statue of San Juan de Ribera, a very effective work by Mariano Benlliure.

The Library maintains its character and preserves some eleven thousand volumes, without forgetting manuscript plays by Lope de Vega. The Library also houses a collection of old protocols, recently formed, with more than 28,000 volumes of great historical value.

A great deal more could be said about the Patriarch's College, its real name being Corpus Christi; more shall be said further on when dealing with the museums.

Courtyard of the Patriarch college, with the statue of San Juan de Ribera.

Patriarch college. The Last Supper by F. Ribalta,
in the main altarpiece of the chapel.

Fine Arts Museum, former college of St. Pius V.

THE FINE ARTS MUSEUM

The Fine Arts Museum, which is installed in the ex college of San Pio V, has been formed from the works gathered together by the San Carlos Academy; works donated by convents in thanks to the said corporation for protecting them, with many others, during the War of Independence; works from mortgage free houses and donated by collectors, Maecenas and other private people. Naturally discounting the Prado Museum, Valencia's Fine Arts Museum, according to some writers, is the second most important pictorically, and, of course, one of the main ones in Spain.

Apart from the quality of the paintings, there is so much in quantity that there is no room here, not even briefly to make any individual references, only a general indication.

Of course, the display of native Valencian artists plays an important part, starting with the well supplied show of the so called «primitive» artists —among them, Dalmau and Jacomart— to go on to the native Valencians or in one form or another followers of the Valencian School, such as Hernando Yañez de la Almedina, Juan de Juanes, the Ribaltas (father and son) Ribera, Espinosa, Jose Vergara, Vicente Lopez and his sons, with whom we come to the resplendent 19th century: Francisco Domingo, Ignacio Pinazo, Muñoz Degrain, Emilio Sala, Jose Benlliure, Joaquin Sorolla (with less works than one could have wished in his own home) and many others, without forgetting Manuel Benedito. Among the painters not connected with the Valencian School, who are represented here, we mention —though not in chronological order— none less than Velazquez (with a famous self-portrait) El Greco, Pinturicchio, Sanchez Coello, Goya (with some of his most qualified portraits), Murillo, Bosco, Morales, Andrea Vaccaro, Madrazo, Bruete, Lopez Mezquita... Some works of these artists come from the important, both in quantity and quality, collection donated by Goerlich-Miquel, which is almost a museum within a museum.

Although the contents of the museum are mainly pictorial, it is not because it lacks sculptures. An especially constructed pavilion displays a good part of the work of Mariano Benlliure (with the original of the mausoleum of the bullfighter Joselito), as well as productions of other sculptors.

Nor is there any sculpture missing from the varied and select archeological section (such as the Iberian sculpture of the lion or lioness by Bocairente).

Fine Arts Museum. One of the rooms dedicated to the Primitive Valencian artists.

Fine Arts Museum «San Vicente», Valencian school (about 1500)
and «San Bruno» by F. Ribalta.

⟵ Altarpiece by Fray Bonifacio Ferrer.

Fine Arts Museum. Self portrait by Velazquez and detail of the portrait of Joaquina Candado by Goya.

THE NATIONAL CERAMICS MUSEUM

Among the monuments in the city of Valencia, one of the most well known in fact and imagination, without doubt, is the palace of the Dukes of Dos Aguas, built in the 15th century by the Rabasas de Perellós, a noble as well as rich family. Half way through the 18th century, this aristocratic abode underwent extensive reforms, following the plans of the original painter Hipolito Rovira, who died a mad man and who decorated the two façades and designed the beautiful fine porch, which was executed by Ignacio Vergara in alabaster stone; the principal motives of this porch are two allegorical figures of the above mentioned title of the Dos Aguas family. In about 1875 another reform was carried out, during which Rovira's paintings disappeared and the building was left, externally, much as it is today, although it should be noted that important consolidation work has been carried out halfway through this century, at the expense of the State, who are now the owners of this building.

The «González Martí» National Ceramics Museum was inaugurated in this building in 1954. It was given this name after the famous ceramics specialist who formed and donated the copious and extremely valuable collection which was to be the nucleus of the Museum, later enlarged.

The said Museum receives numerous visitors as the contents of its many halls are of interest to both the well informed as well as the simply curious public. Eith regard to the ceramics themselves, there is a rich voluminous representation from the big Valencian centres of Paterna, Manises and Alcora; productions from many periods, from Iberian times to Picasso; genuinely Spanish pieces —Talavera, Sevilla, Toledo— and pieces from China and Japan, for example; rooms which invite study, such as the room of medieval tiles and the singular socorrats, and also spectacular rooms, such as the kitchen or the one with the porcelain chairs; exquisite things such as a «Rondeau» by Benedetto de Maiano and popular things such as anecdotal compositions.

From some years now, the Museum has been enlarging its programme to include works belonging to the decorative arts in general —not forgetting a sumptuous carriage used by the Dos Aguas family—, as well as dedicating rooms for enhancing certain personnages.

77

Fine Arts Museum. «La Piedad», board painting by Rodrigo de Osona (15th cent.) and «Martyrdom of St. Sebastian» by Jose Ribera.

Façade of the Palace of the Marquis of Dos Aguas.

National Museum of Pottery. «Socarrat» from Paterna (15th century

Paleontological Museum installed in the Almudín.

Detail of the altarpiece by Fray Bonifacio Ferrer.
Fine Arts Museum. Baptism of Christ.

Cathedral. Main altarpiece.
Presentation of the Virgin in the Temple
by Yañez de la Almedina and H. Llanos.

OTHER NON RELIGIOUS MUSEUMS

Jose Rodrigo y Botet, a Valencian who left for the Argentine in 1842, acquired there a large paleontological collection. Although he could have sold it for a good price, he donated it to Valencia. The collection was installed in the old Almudin or flour deposit, a very curious building built in the 16th century which, according to Hugo Obermaier, is ideal for a Paleontological Museum. This is an extremely important Museum, as there is no other like it in Europe with so much American Quaternary material, unless we consider —improbably— the ones in Paris or London. This is because it contains a series of unique pieces in the world and because it houses a portion of the most complete and best preserved skeletons of the same species to be found in other museums.

The Prehistoric Museum, as well as the Prehistoric Investigation Service, were both founded in 1927 by the Provincial Deputation. They have been adequately installed since 1955 in the Bailia palace. The Museum occupies ten rooms, in which many selected pieces, from the paleolitic to the Roman period, are displayed; the remains of the skull of a man from Neanderthal; thousands of flagstones engraved in the Franco-Cantabric art style; cardial ceramics, which form an unequalled collection in Spain; the country's richest collection of Iberian epigraphy; Iberian ceramics from Livia, which are as artistically suggestive as valuable for getting to know a civilization, etc. Special mention should be made to the American prehistoric collection donated by Ruben Vela, one of the most considerable in Europe. With regard to the Prehistoric Investigation Service, more than three hundred excavations and prospections have been carried out by them and they also publish monographs and year-books, describing the works carried out.

The Municipal Historic Museum occupies various rooms in the City's House. This museum houses the 13th century Banner of the Conquest; the Senyera, Valencia's representative flag; a sword attributed to Don Jaime the Conqueror; the codexes of the privileges and the Consolat de Mar; the oldest letter of exchange in Spain; the Taula de Canvis, the first bank to exist in Valencia (1407); objects from the extinguished guilds; objects of art, curiosities, etc.

The Bullfighting Museum, which houses numerous old and modern objects, is the first of a public nature to be installed in Spain. It is at the moment being reinstalled.

— Patriarch College. Virgin with Child (16th cent.).

Prehistory Museum. Iberian Horseman. Bronze.

Prehistory Museum. Display window with exvotes and Iberian ceramics,
and detail of the iberian vase «of the warriors» of Liria.

RUPESTRIAN PAINTING IN THE LEVANTE DISTRICT

In the previous chapter dedicated to the Prehistoric Museum, the Rupestrian paintings displayed there in adequate reproductions with regard to colour and size, were not mentioned. It would be a good idea, therefore, to dedicate some attention here to this extraordinary artistic manifestation.

If one cannot literally take for granted all that has been said regarding the fact that the Rupestrian paintings, discovered in land now forming part of the province of Valencia, were forerunners of the skill in the cultivation of art later shown by the people of Valencia themselves, it is possible to adopt some words said by Professor Lafuente Ferrari. Consequently we can write that in the field of the historical-geographical sphere called the Kingdom of Valencia or the Valencien Region, «there are vestiges of pictorical art of great interest dating from very remote times».

The said adjective is applied to the afore-mentioned Rupestrian painting because it is found on the rocks, not in more or less deep dark caves, but in mountain shelters. To apply the work «levantine» to that painting, as usually happens, seems to be justified —which is not always the case when applying this denomination at other times— because it is not only found in lands belonging to day to Valencia, but also in Cataluña, Southern Aragon, in the province of Albacete...

In the same way as the Altamira paintings and everything connected with same only present isolated figures of animals, expressed with marvellous realism, this Levantine Rupestrian painting is of a no means less marvellous impressionism or expressionism and offers representations of the human figure and compositions: the collecting of a honey by a woman; another woman with basket in hand; archers shooting arrows at a herd of deer; hunting other animals; a parade of warriors, etc.

The most important nucleus of the Valencian Rupestrian paintings is in the province of Castellon (Barranco de la Gassulla, in Ares del Maestre, with representations of bovines, boar and goats; Barranco de Valltorta, between Albocacer and Tirig, with hundreds of figures; Morella la Vella, Puebla de Benifazá and Borriol). In the province of Valencia, there are paintings at Dos Aguas, with the Cinto de las Letras and the Cinto de la Ventana; Ayora, with El Sordo and La Tortosilla, and Bicorp, with the Cueva de la Araña. In the province of Alicante, we should mention Alcoy, with La Sarga.

The chronology of these paintings has been the object of much discussion. Professor Martin Almagro dates them as more less 3,000 B. C. However, from a certain point of view, the seem so modern...!

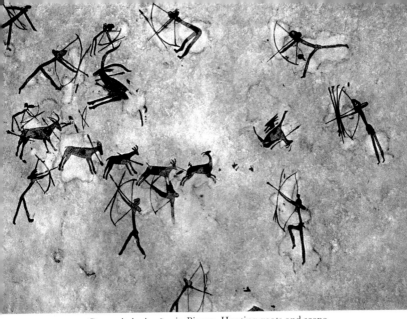

Cueva de la Araña, in Bicorp. Hunting goats and scene
from the collection of honey.

RELIGIOUS MUSEUMS

Cardinal Enrique Reig inaugurated an Archeological Dioscesan Museum in 1922, installed in the Archbishop's Palace. The very rich contents of that museum were either destroyed or dispersed in a great part in 1936. With what was recovered and some other contributions, the Diocesan Archeological Museum was reorganized as from 1956 and installed in the former Seminary, occupying several rooms. Room I (Romanic-Gothic) is the most interesting with numerous works by the Primitive artists, in paintings and carvings. Room II (Orrente) contains eight canvases, with biblical scenes, attributed by some to the afore-mentioned Murcian painter. Room III (Renaissance) displays works of a certain variety. Room IV (17th and 18th centuries) corresponds quite simply to the said chronological indication.

The Cathedral Museum is installed in several chapels and other parts of the church itself. It contains numerous paintings by the Primitives (Osona, father, Pere Nicolau Marçal de Sax, etc.); local Renaissance (Osona son, Hernando de Llanos and Hernando Yáñez de la Almedina, Juanes and his father) Italian and Burgundy schools; the dark period and following styles and more recent authors, such as Goya, with two large canvases connected with San Francisco de Borja. In sculpture, we pick out a polychromed wood altarpiece of the Death and Assumption of the Virgin (14th century) and twelve reliefs, already mentioned by Jualiano Florentino (beginning of the 16th century). With regard to the gold and silver work, we should mention a pax attributed to Benvenuto Cellini and the processional monstrance, a recent work, by various artists, which is 4 meters high and is made of silver (some 600 kgs.), with gold, platinum and precious stones.

The Patriarch Museum has been in existence since 1954 and is installed in the chapel of the Purisima and several adjacent rooms, which have been suitably equipped. In the said chapel, we should point out a beautiful sculpture of the Virgin in polychromed wood, by Gregorio Fernandez or his school and twelve magnificent Flemish tapestries of the 16th century. With regard to the contents of the new rooms, we should mention in the first place four Grecos: «The Adoration of the shepherds», «St. Francis of Asissi with the skull», an allegorical picture with two figures and a vellum with the «Dream of St. Martin». The tryptych of «The Crucifiction, the Descent and the Resurrection», by Roger van der Weyden or —according to Elias Tormo— Tierry Bouts, is worthy of note. There are also works by Juanes, his family or school, Luis de Morales, Francisco Ribalta, etc., as well as embroidery, stained glass, codexes and curiosities.

The miracle of the Virgen del Rosario del «Caballeros de Colonia» probably the work of Monso, disciple of Pablo de San Leocadia.

Patriarch college. Chapel of the Purisima or of the Monument.

Cathedral. «Piedad», by H. Yañez de la Almedina.

⟵ Patriarch college. Tryptych attributed to Thierry Bouts (15th cent.).

MONUMENTS

The number of monuments of homage or remembrance in the City of Valencia is so great that even a simple list of them would not fit into one page of this book, therefore we shall mention only a few.

The one dedicated to San Pedro Pascual, a Mozarab Valencian who was bishop of Jaen, is the work of Tomas Llorens, of the 17th century and is situated on the river embankment.

Mariano Benlliure is the author of monuments to San Juan de Ribera (in the cloister of the Patriarch College), to the painter Jose Ribera, Cervantes, the Marquis de Campo —restorer-mayor of the Valencian capital and company man—, to the painter Francisco Domingo and Joaquin Sorolla (only the bust). Some of these works are the author's best.

One of the most important monuments, for its own sake and one account of its situation in the Parterre, is the one dedicated to Jaime the Conqueror, by Agapito Vallmitjana. El Cid is remembered in the famous equestrian statue by Ana Hyat Huntington, donated by the artist herself.

Sculpture and architectonic volumes form an excellent ensemble in the ALAMEDA in the monument to Dr. Moliner, phthisist and politician. Author: Jose Capuz.

The fraternal poets Teodoro Llorente and Vicente Wenceslao Querol are also depicted among the trees in statues by Gabriel Borras and Jose Arnal respectively.

Among the recently erected monuments, there are ones dedicated to the Head of State, the Generalisimo Franco, by Jose Capuz; Vicente Domenech, el Palleter, hero of the War of Independence, by Emilio Calandin; Juan Luis Vives, with a bust of the humanis sculpted by Ramon Mateu; the musician Jose Serrano, with statue and sculpted frieze by Octavio Vicent...

Octavio Vicent is also the author of statues representing Valencia, the rector Vicente Blasco —an eminent reformer of higher studies—, Alexander VI, Ferdinand and Isabel, in a monumental fountain attached to the former University building. We should also mention among others the fountain dedicated to Mariano Benlliure, in the El Carmen district, with a bronze reproduction of a delightful group of children playing, by the artist himself.

Finally we mention the large number of reverential or remembrance monuments, such as the typical ceramic altarpieces.

Monument to Jose Ribera by Mariano Benlliure. —

Monument to Maestro Serrano by Octavio Vicent.

N. SEÑORA DE CONSOLACION. AÑO 1786

AVE MARIA PURISIMA SIN PECADO CONCEBIDA

One of the numerous ceramic altarpieces which embellish
the streets of Valencia.

Pompous baroque style in the porch of the Dos Aguas Palace. ⟶

Rice plants between white houses and blue irrigation canals.

← Central Market, noisy bustle.

MARKETS AND LOCAL MARKETS

For many centuries, Valencia's main market was famous not only in the rest of Spain but also abroad, to judge by the enthusiastic descriptions of the Countess of Gasparin and other travellers. This fame was founded both in the veracity of the products offered for sale as well as in the motley crowd which thronged between the polychromed stalls of quickly changing goods under white awnings, keeping off the rays of the sun. With regard to the rest of the market, there were specialized areas where birds, beef and veal, salt meat, etc. were sold respectively, there always being a spot for the sale of flowers, which was the origin of the existing street of Ramilletes. The Market Square was also the scene of horse tournaments and bullfights, as well as the temporary or permanent site for the gallows.

Well into this century this market still preserved some of its typical characteristics; but in 1915 the first stone was laid for the Central Market which was inaugurated in 1928, after extensive works, which included excavations giving rise to archeological finds.

Francisco Guardia Vidal and Alejandro Soler y March were the architects of the project. The building cost five and a half million pesetas. Several materials, including a great deal of iron, were included in the work. The building is of an irregular shape, consisting of two bodies, the smaller one being dedicated to the fish section. The number of posts amounts to more than 1,300. From the technical point of view, it has been said that it is one of the best markets in Europe. It is, of course, a centre of tourist attraction.

There are complementary markets in different points of the city —Colon, Ruzafa, Botanico, Cabañal— built in accordance with modern requirements. However, there are still a few open air markets with their pleasant picturesque airs.

Finally we should mention the Provisions Market or Contracting Exchange between fruit and vegetable wholesalers and retailers. It was begun in 1940, planned by the architect Javier Goerlich, and was finished several years later. It is of a functional nature, with typical notes of the architecture of the locality.

THE VOICE OF THE BELLS

Just as all the men in the world tend to dress in the same way, all the cities in the world tend to be similar, with square houses and streets drawn out in a straight line. However, Valencia still preserves a certain variety within its shell, as can be seen from visiting certain districts.

The Cathedral district is an example of this fact, as it spreads around the said church. Close to the Cathedral is the new Archbishop's palace, a brilliant work by the architect Traver, and the Royal Basilica of Our Lady of the Helpless, its interior being of an elyptical shape and the vault magnificently painted al fresco by Palomino and a 15th century adorned image of the Virgin of that invocation, the Patron of Valencia and its Kingdom. In this same area there are the churches of the Saviour, with an impressive Christ of the Cross; the church of San Esteban, with elegant baroque decoration, where —according to tradition or legend— El Cid's daughters were married and where the font is preserved in which San Vicente Ferrer, also Patron of Valencia and kingdom, was baptized. The church of St. Nicholas, with its excellent al fresco vault painted by Dionis Vidal, altarpiece by Osona, interesting plaques by Juanes and gold and silver work donated by the Borja family, as Calixto III was not rector of this parish for nothing; the church of Santa Catalina, recently restored in its ogival style and bell tower (by Juan Bautista Viñes in the 18th century), considered as the most beautiful of the baroque towers is Spain; the church of San Martin, which preserves in the niche in its façade a bronze group of St. Martin, which is considered a masterpiece of the sculptured art of the primitive Flemish painters... But, putting aside other churches, we must refer to the Calle de los Caballeros because, apart from the already described palace of the Generalidad, it contains a certain number of aristocratic mansions with wide typical entrances, made to measure for the carriages, and the former can be seen in nearby streets under the solemn chime of the bells...

The Market district, around this great supply centre, contains the parish church of the St. Johns, for the vault of which Palomino magnificently painted perhaps the biggest composition in Europe; it contains streets named after various guilds: Tundidores (Cloth Shearers), Bolsería (manufacture of bags, etc.), Zurradores (Leather dressers), Tapicería (Taspestry), shops with goods on the street, which date from when there were illiterates. The district smells of toasted coffee and spices; this is where the painter Joaquin Sorolla was born (in the Calle de las Mantas) and the novelist Blasco Ibañez (in the no longer existing street of la Jabonería Nueva).

⊩— Santa Catalina Tower (18th cent.).

Basilica of the Virgin of the Helpless. Cupola painted
by A. Palomino.

Church of St. Martín. Sculptured group of the saint. (15th cent.).

Detail of the vault painted by Palomino.

St. Nicholas. Chalice called after Calixto III

Church of St. Nicholas. Small altarpiece with Limoge enamels.

Church of St. Nicholas. «Crucifiction», painted on board by
Maestro Rodrigo de Osona, Sr. (1476).

Admirals Palace. Courtyard. ⟶

Bailia Palace's courtyard.

⟵ Escriva family palace.

BOOKS, BULLS AND SILKS

The University district, apart from containing the already described building, the also already mentioned pedagogic foundation of San Juan de Ribera and another foundation —materially disfigured at the moment— of Santo Tomas de Villanueva, also contains the Pouet de Sant Vicent or Birthplace of the Saint, reconstructed in the neo-gothic style by the architect Vicente Valls with superb 18th century scenic tiles, the church of St. Thomas the Apostle and San Felipe Neri, the latter being known as such because the church was an Oratory, one of the worshippers being the distinguished mathematician, P. Tosca, who perhaps planned the building in the 18th century; the church which was the parish priory for the order of San Juan del Hospital, a work of the 13th and 14th centuries and worthy of a better destiny. Apart from other churches, the district also contains the Baños del Almirante (Admiral's Baths), one of the few examples of the Arab occupation which still exist in Valencia. Old and new book shops, as well as antique shops all add to the quaint character of this district.

The Ruzafa district had a great deal of personality as it was not for nothing an independent municipality from the city until it was annexed to same in 1877. It has lost the country atmosphere, as it is now completely modernized but it still maintains a certain bullfighting fame, as many matadors were born there —among them the almost legendary bullfighter Julio «Fabrilo»—. It also contains Valencia's bullring, one of the principal ones in Spain on account of its architecture and magnificence The Ruzafa church of San Valero paying court to the baroque bell tower...

The Silk district was given this name as it was the main nucleus of the silk industry; it is sufficient to say that in 1876, right in the middle of the period of decadence, 103 industrialists of this branch worked in this district in comparison with 56 of the rest of the population. In this area we find the College of Silk Fine Arts, a beautiful building with very interesting contents; the emblazoned mansion of the Tamarit family, aristocratic manufacturers who in the 18th century had 300 employees, and the ostentatious bourgeois house of Joaquin Manuel Fos, a very important promoter of this industry during the same century. This district can be divided into several sections such as the Hospital district, which is preserved in part, the Pilar district, after the church of this name, and the Escuelas Pías district, with the college whose circular church displays under the blue skies a magnificent cupula of by no means less blue tiles.

Three aspects of the College of Higher silk art.

Fountain and well of the house where San Vicente Ferrer was born.

Arab baths.

Cloister of Santo Domingo.

ON THE BANKS OF THE RIVER

The El Carmen district is perhaps the purest of them all, taking this in the highest sense of word. Its name is derived from the fact that there was a Carmelite convent there, their church being known as Santa Cruz —today the Parish church—. The fact that this district housed until very recently the Royal Academy of San Carlos of Fine Arts and the Higher School of Painting, Sculpture and Engraving, as well as the still existing school of Arts and Crafts, naturally influences the great number of artisans and artists who are trained and who work in this district. Juan de Juanes lived there; Mariano Benlliure was born there. Furthermore, it is a district of secluded streets, in which mansions alternate with modest «escaleta» or step houses, the ground floors of which are used by house carvers, guilders, or for fan painting workshops, restoration of antiques, kite manufacture and other crafts. Several ceramic tiles in the walls speak of guilds and popular devotions...

The two banks of the River Turia, on its course through the city of Valencia, belong, as is natural, due to its length, to different districts, which need not be listed.

On the right bank, we should note several small gardens along the embankments; the Temple, priory convent of the Montesa Order, today the Civil Government Headquarters, whilst the church next door belongs to the Redemptionist Fathers, all constructed during the reign of Charles III, and the various subsisting buildings of which the building of Santo Domingo was most important. The most modern building is the Capitanía General. The oldest part is of positive architectonic value, especially the capitular chamber, in ogival style, with exceedingly elegant columns, the also Gothic cloister, which has been recently successfully restored, and the Kings' Chapel (15th century), of constructive virtuosity, also containing the beautiful marble tomb of the Marqueses of Zenete; we should not forget either the chapel of San Vicente Ferrer (18th century).

On the left bank, we should point out the little known but worth visiting Trinity convent, where the Middle Ages still seem to slumber and which contains the tomb of the wife of Alfonso the Magnanimous; the already mentioned museum of St. Pius V; the Real and Alameda gardens; the very modern indoor swimming pool and the by no means less modern Archives of the Kingdom of Valencia, the work of the architect Segura de Lago, who has provided a very suitable shelter for the opulent documentary treasure.

Capitular chamber of Santo Domingo church. ⟶

Front gate of the Palace of the Dukes of Mandas, close
to the Fine Arts Museum.

Santo Domingo. King's Chapel. ⟶

ON THE SEA FRONT

One of the most extensive districts of Valencia is the seafront one. Some of the names of its different sectors are: Cantarranas, el Grao, el Cabañal, el Canyamelar, la Malvarrosa...

Here we can easily recall Valencia's sea tradition, which is much more important than is generally imagined. In this respect, it is significant that a short time after the conquest, the king Pedro the Great, the conqueror's son, had as many Valencian as Catalan galleys for his expedition to Tunis. It is by no means less significant that Valencia should establish, through a special privilege of the same King Pedro in 1283, the famous marine tribune Consolat de Mar, before Palma de Mallorca, Barcelona, Perpignan, etc. The capital itself repeatedly contributed to shipping companies, at times against corsairs and pirates, although they did not receive the help which seemed indicated.

Valencia disposed of the corresponding arsenals for their marine activities. Through a municipal agreement dated 1338, the majority were built in el Grao. They were used as such until the 18th century, when with the loss of Valencia's privileges, they were dedicated by Philip V's representatives to other services. However, the five big architectonic naves still exist, with their ogival arches, in which plans are being made for installing a Sea Museum. For the rest, vessels of more or less tonnage are built on the nearby beaches and modern ships of different types are constructed in the shipyards of the Union Naval de Levante.

With regard to the port, this is a demontration of the fact that the people of Valencia, written off at times as inconstant and improvisers, sometimes know how to persist in such arduous tasks as the construction of wharfs and docks in unfavourable circumstances, until the present result was reached.

Apart from the above, this district although it is not impervious to reforms and improvements, still preserves a certain air about its clean gay little houses, as well as about its spirited and —naturally— «Salty» inhabitants...

The Yacht Club, the beaches and the numerous beach restaurants with their rice dishes and shell fish, respectively facilitate sport, summer holidays and the not to be disdained gastronomic satisfactions.

◄— Torre Valencia.

— Effect of the sun on the Albufera.

One aspect of the shipyards.

Loading crate of oranges.

Partial view of the Club Nautico.

THE ALBUFERA AND ITS PASTURELAND

The Albufera, in the municipal boundary of Valencia, is a lake —or to be more exact a penelake— formed in remote times by springs and especially by sweet water streams which were contained very close to the sea by sandbars. During the Roman era, the Albufera —which was not then known as such as it is an Arab name— covered in modern terms some 30,000 hectares which are now reduced to some 3,000 due to natural destruction and especially to the vigorous action of the riverside people who aspired to gaining this land for growing rice, which is characteristic of this area.

The Albufera is separated from the Mediterranean by the Dehesa (Pastureland), a long and relatively narrow strip of pine trees and low hills which in the past were hunting grounds for deer, wild boar, hares, partridges and other animals and which still housed more or less savage bulls in the 19th century. A project has been recently put into action for converting this site —where there is a national highway inn with a golf course— into one of the most important tourist complexes in Europe.

The most interesting aspect of the lake is derived in the first place from the landscape, the perspectives of which —the water like a huge silver lake, the vegetation which springs up here and there, the purple reflections of the sun— make the spectator feel he has been transported to the Far East. The Albufera is also interesting because it still determines a good part of the human life in its surrounds, although this has changed a good deal since the novel Cañas y Barro was written.

The fishing of eels, as well as grigs, together with several other types of fish, is one of the forms of exploiting the Albufera; but it is more famous for the special shoots held there of water birds, which are as numerous as they are varied. The «tirades», as the shoots are usually called, amount to twenty odd in the season, which lasts from September to March. These shoots have not only been attended by numerous kings —from Juan I the Hunter to Alfonso XIII— but also by many other influential or popular personnages, including the famous bullfighter Rafael Gomez Ortega. The latter had such a good aim that he put his rivals' supporters' noses out of join when they said: «El Gallo doesn't kill».

128

Fisherman on the Albufera, pushing the «barquet». ⟶

Aspects of the Albufera and surrounds.

THE ORCHARD AND ITS DWELLINGS

The city of Valencia, apart from having been the capital of the former kingdom of the same name (historical value) and from being the capital of the province of the same name (administrative value), is also the head of a district called la Huerta or Orchard (geographical value).

Valencia's Huerta is a plain, splendidly cultivated in general, some 27km. long by some 11 wide, between its most distant points which are: Puzol to the north, with reference to Catarroja to the south, and Manises to the West, with reference to Malvarrosa beach to the east. This plain has been assimilated to an irregular isosceles triangle, the base of which is the sea and the vertex the River Turia, between Paterna and the aforementioned town of Manises.

Foreign authors have always praised this Huerta for its pleasant aspect and its fertility. The historian Juan de Mariana, for example, after describing in his own way the said land, said nothing less than: «such were the Elysian Plains, paradise and delling place of the blessed, as referred to by the ancient poets».

It is of course true that the city of Valencia is expanding at the cost of the orchard lands. But apart from the fact that this is being compensated by the increase of irrigation systems, the Huerta still preserves many of its attractions, among them the cottages and farmhouses.

The cottage or barraca is a dwelling of probable palafitte origin, which proves its very remote origin. It was of course built with local materials: the walls with bricks made of clays and rice shells; the roof with cane framework to which the brushwood of different species were attached from the Albufera or surrounds. This produced a functional, clean and comfortable dwelling, which has been praised by the poet Llorente and popularized by the novelist Blasco Ibañez.

The alqueria or farmhouse has been less lucky in this respect. This is more of an architectonic structure, which was usually both the dwelling for the lords of the manor as well as for the farm labourers. Carved stone was often used in the construction. The existing examples are valuable witnesses of the Gothic and baroque styles.

Orchard cottages. ►─◄

Cultivation of tomatoes close to the city.

THE FAMOUS GARDENS

What a great garden and floral tradition there is in Valencia...! This tradition goes back even further than the Muslem rule. Al-Makkai, who was not from Valencia, wrote: «the abundance of gardens makes Valencia the bouquet of Spain; its Ruzafa (a name which, as we have seen, is still used for a certain district of the city) is considered as one of the most charming dwellings on earth».

After the Christian reconquest, Peter the Ceremonious classified the Valencian jasmins as big and wide (grans e amples); Martin the Humane requested Valencian jasmins for planting in his Barcelona palace; Alfonso the Magnanimous called for Valencian gardeners for creating and looking after the orchards and gardens in the kingdom of Naples; Ferdinand the Catholic king, installed with his wife in the Alcazar in Sevilla, requested the General Council of Valencia to send gardeners, trees and shrubs for that residence...

Meanwhile, the great gardens of the royal palace were being formed in the capital, where there was a zoo already in the 15th century, with lions, camels, bears, gazelles, and elk, etc. A similar garden sein exists, naturally very much changed, under the name of the Real pardens or less appropriately Viveros Municipales or Nursery gardens.

The 18th century shows a blooming —a word never more appropriately used— of gardens. The Alameda gardens, still existing today, must also be attributed to this century. The Mayor suchet introduced improvements, which were praised in verse by Leandro Fernandez de Moratin, at the time when he was resident in the Valencian capital.

The 19th century was responsible for the Glorieta, which had a tropical note with bamboos, cherimoyas and banana trees, and the Parterre, which it has been said sings for the childrens to go there. The neo-classical garden of Monforte was formed in the 19th century and in 1941 it was officially declared an Artistic Garden.

For the rest the city —with the famous Botanical Garden— continues to adorn itself with garden streets and corners brightened with plants and flowers.

All this is without counting the gardens and orchards and especially the orange groves. It was not in vain that cardinal de Retz, that turbulent French personage of the 18th century, wrote in his travel memoires «From Aragon, I entered the Kingdom of Valencia, which can be considered as not only the healthiest spot, but also the most beautiful garden in the world».

Glorieta Garden.

Real Gardens.

Botanical Garden.

Another aspect of the Botanical Garden.

THE TYPICAL DRESS

The visitor to the capital of Valencia has the opportunity at certain times and in certain circumstances, to admire the women, generally young girls, dressed in the brilliant polychromed dress, which was born in the past on holidays by the well-to-do peasant women.

In this respect, the most impressive display is held in about the middle of March, consisting of an offer of flowers to the Virgin of the Unprotected, the patron saint of the City, for which a procession is organized through the streets of thousands of girls dressed in these costumes. They can also be seen in smaller groups at other festivities and solemnities throughout the year. For sometime now it was not been unrare for a girl to go to the altar dressed in this costume, although the multi-colours are exchanged for pure white.

Jose Ortega and Gasset was not stritcly correct when he wrote in his prologue to Ortiz Echangue's book «Tipos y trajes de España»: «The costume of the ordinary woman in Aragon and Valencia is the costume of an 18th century lady executed in poor materials by rouch craftsmen». Poor materials in the typical costumes of the Valencian women? It is precisely the opposite... Bartolome Joly, adviser to the King of France, wrote after a trip in 1603: «There isn't as much curiosity, magnificence or pomp, in dress in the whole of Spain as there is in Valencia. Elegance is a natural element there and even the crafts people dress in silks». When we say craftsmen we mean the wives and daughters of the 17th to 19th century workers, who were precisely the ones to look after the silkworm.

There is a great deal more to be said —and it has been said— about this female costume, completed by the headpiece, which the Countess of Pardo Bazan compaired with that of the Lady of Elche; but it would be a good idea to dedicate a few words to the costumes of the old Valencian labourers, which they wore on feast days or to ceremonies. It did not consist of the open shirt and breeches, but of other pieces made in rich materials such as silk and velvet in black and bright colours. What a pity it has not been preserved!

Valencian girls wearing traditional costume. ⟶

Grace and charm of the traditional costume.

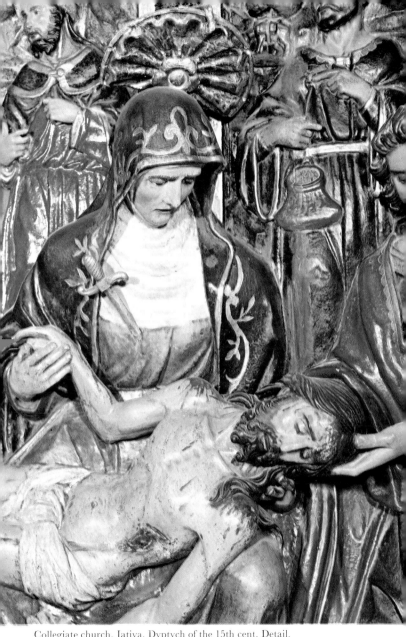

Collegiate church. Jativa. Dyptych of the 15th cent. Detail.

One of the 1967 Fallas, referring to horoscopes. ➤

Paella: the very famous Valencian dish.

Typical kitchen in the National Ceramics Museum.

THE FALLAS

Among the numerous festivals held in the City of Valencia, the Fallas are worthy of note for various reasons. A «fallas» means here a bonfire or a type of «Guy» which is an artistic-satirical monument, built in the streets a few days before the feast of St. Joseph and which are lit up and burnt on the night of 19th to 20th March.

The origin of the Fallas is probably to be found in a certain custom of the carpinters living in the capital, as at the beginning of the spring, before the official date of same, they used to burn in the streets or squares the devices which were no longer serviceable and which had been used to lighting during the long winter nights. Then they began to add to the shapeless mounds rough rag dolls (ninots), which in turn were given burlesque touch to amuse the neighbours. The appearance of these dolls was improved at the same time the range of their allusions and criticisms increased.

In general terms, the birth of the Fallas can be situated in the 18th century; the development and specialization of its character in the 19th century and perfection in this century. Throughout the 19th century, the municipal authorities adopted very diverse attitudes towards the Fallas; but, in 1901, the City Council very decidedly took the part of protecting them, by means of a prize, since then multiplied.

In 1946 the Fallas were declared a Festival of national artistic interest and in 1965 a Festival of Tourist interest, by the respective ministries. The number of Fallas amounts to some 150, costing several million pesetas.

All the Fallas are burnt on the afore-mentioned night, amidst displays of pyrotechnics and the jubilation of thousands of local and outside people. A little later the wooden, cardboard etc. monuments, which cost so much money and effort, are reduced to ashes.., not without having provided earnings to the artists or craftsmen, industrialists, merchants and another others directly or indirectly connected with the fallas. In brief, Maurice Legendre also said: «By reducing more than 100 fallas to ashes, Valencia makes us understand how easy and how disinterestedly they can create beauty».

The complicated erection of a «falla».

Falla referring to the excesses of propaganda. ➞

Detail of a falla : «juerga» for tourists.

The culminating moment of the «fallas»: «La crema».

GASTRONOMY

The city of Valencia is the centre of an area which, from the gastronomic point of view is characterized mainly by the «paella». The people of Valencia give this name to a type of frying pan, which has no handle and which is relatively low, and also to the dish they cook in it. This consists of rice with chicken (when it is not fish and shellfish), certain vegetables and spicies. A normal recipe would not be sufficient for obtaining a good dish of paella if the cook, professional or amateur, was not aware of a few tips for obtaining two very important points: that the rice is just right —neither hard nor soft— and that the grains should be quite loose and not stuck together. It was not in vain that Jose Maria Peman wrote these two lines, among many others, about the paella: «Oh liberal dish where each grain is a grain —just as each man is one vote!»

The paella —which until quite recently was only a dish for local or regional consumption— has lately acquired an incredibly extensive and intensive prestige, on an international range. Dr. Marañon, for example, wrote in 1952: «one of the greatest surgeons in the States recently confided in me that he would exchange the whole of the Prado Museum for a paella such as the one he had just eaten in Valencia...»

Other rice dishes can be eaten in the City of Valencia, apart from those which constitute the speciality of other Valencian districts. But those who like strongly characteristic dishes, can try preferably in the Albufera area, the all-i-pebre (garlic and pepper) for dressing with corresponding sauce the eels, which are also very tasty prepared a l'ast, i.e. speared in skewers over a preferably aromatic wood fire.

Refreshments such as the orgeat of chufas —when it maintains its authenticity up against the sudden propaganda attacks of certain exotic refreshments—, certain sweets such as oranges and strawberries (separately or in a delicious combination), sweets such as turron or sugar almonds, not to mention less permanent or less generalized things, all make up the varied extensive gastronomic panorama, which can be «contemplated» in the Valencian capital.

Elaboration of the buñuelos during the fiestas of San Jose. →

Tea time in a garden. Tile picture in the National ceramics Museum.

Valencia. Arenas Beach.

Saler Beach.

THE AZAHAR COAST

From a Tourist point of view, the city of Valencia is situated in the officially called Azahar or Orange Blossom Coast, which covers the provinces of Castellon and Valencia. Most of this shore is cultivated, each time more extensively, with orange trees, the tree with the pernnial leaves, which in winter bears its golden fruit and in the spring its white sweet smelling blossom, after which the Coast has been named.

From north to south of this coastline, there are attractive townships such as: Vinaroz, famous for its prawns; Benicarlo, close by; Peñiscola, the historic and picturesque peninsula, where Pope Luna took refuge; Oropesa, with its Torre del Rey, a model of military architecture; Benicasim, a tourist resort; Castellon de la Plana, a rapidly expanding city; Burriana, one of the main orange ports... All these towns are in the province of Castellon.

Now in the province of Valencia, the Azahar coast continues to offer excellent beaches —some of them not yet exploited from a tourist point of view— and such interesting towns like El Puig; with a great Mercedarian cenoby in which History and Art echo; the Valencian capital and suburbs, the main object of this book; Cullera, rich and picturesque, close to the mouth of the river Jucar; Oliva, which ends the itinerary with a white, green and blue smile...

Gandia is a lively flourishing town, the home of the great poet Ausias March and St. Francisco of Borja, who was Duke of Gandia. The Duke's palace is carefully preserved and can be visited. There is a great deal of activity in the port of Gandia, mostly with regard to the export of oranges. Its vast, peaceful beach, with its excellent hotel, is becoming more and more popular each year.

With regard to Jativa, this is situated inland, in the middle of a fertile district. It is the town of the Spanish popes Calixto III and Alejandro VI. It still preserves, from its castle to its blazoned houses, in a large part its old flavour. Its collegiate church is of large proportions. We should also mention the hermitage of San Felix. The numerous continually spouting fountains are one of the charms of the ancient Setabis.

Cullera. Beach

Sagunto. Entrance door to the Roman Theatre.

Sagunto. General view of the Roman Theatre, Museum and Castle.

Jativa. Font of holy water in the Hermitage of San Felix
and end Cross in the Museum.

Castle.

Gandia. Beach, urban view and Duke's Palace.

The Virgin of the Helpless, Patron Saint of the City
and Kingdom of Valencia

INFORMACIÓN PRÁCTICA VALENCIA

INFORMATION PRATIQUE VALENCIA

PRACTICAL INFORMATION VALENCIA

PRAKTISCHE INFORMATION VALENCIA

La mayor parte de estos datos han sido facilitados por la Delegación de Información y Turismo de Valencia. Información puesta al día el 24-2-71.

La plupart de ces renseignements a été fournie par la Délégation d'Information et de Tourisme Valencia. Information mise à jour le 24-2-71.

The majority of these facts have been supplied by the Valencia Delegation of Information and Tourism. Information brought up to date 24-2-71.

Der grösste Teil der Daten wurde von der Delegation für Information und Turismus in Valencia zur Verfügung gestellt. Die Information wurde am 24-2-71 auf den neuesten Stand gebracht.

VALENCIA, con 10.763 Km.² de extensión y 1.574.712 habitantes, es una de las provincias más prósperas y características del Levante español. Fundamentalmente agrícola, produce, sobre todo, arroz y agrios. La naranja valenciana tiene renombre universal. Desde el punto de vista industrial, Valencia ha sabido adecuar su artesanía a los nuevos tiempos, incrementando las típicas manufacturas de muebles, cueros, cerámicas y sedas.

Las industrias más importantes son las de papel, cemento y electricidad. Hay altos hornos en Sagunto, unos grandes astilleros en el puerto de Valencia e industrias metalúrgicas de gran importancia.

El clima, sin grandes oscilaciones, mantiene una temperatura cálida a lo largo de la mayor parte del año.

Una buena red de comunicaciones —carreteras, vías férreas, aeropuerto y puerto— sitúan a Valencia a la cabeza de las capitales españolas.

Son poblaciones importantes: Sagunto —famosa ya en la antigüedad—, Liria —centro musical de la provincia—, Cullera y Gandía —centros turísticos de gran importancia—, Carcagente —destacado centro naranjero—, Játiva, Sueca, Alcira, Requena, etc.

El folklore, muy brillante, adquiere su máxima expresión en las «fallas» del día de San José. Es una fiesta bulliciosa, en la que se conjugan el fuego, la música y el buen humor. Es igualmente famosa la Feria de Julio.

Valencia capital, con 583.151 habitantes, es una hermosa ciudad de carácter mediterráneo, alegre y luminosa; con importantes monumentos, entre los que destacan el palacio del Marqués de Dos Aguas, La Lonja, El Miguelete, la catedral, los museos Provincial de Bellas Artes, Nacional de Cerámica «González Martí», Paleontológico y el de Prehistoria.

La región valenciana ha dado a la cocina española su plato más conocido en el mundo: la paella, especialidad de sinfonía gastronómica sobre el arroz.

VALENCE, avec 10.763 Km.² et 1.574.712 habitants, est l'une des provinces les plus caractéristiques du Levant espagnol. Fondamentalement agricole, elle produit surtout du riz et des agrumes. L'orange valencienne jouit d'une renommée universelle. Du point de vue industriel, Valence a su adapter son artisanat aux temps nouveaux et ses manufactures typiques de meubles, de cuirs, de céramique et de soieries ont pris un nouvel essor.

Les industries les plus importantes sont celles du papier, du ciment et de l'électricité. Citons aussi les hauts-fourneaux de Sagunto, les chantiers navals de port de Valence ainsi que les industries métallurgiques.

Le climat ne présente pas de grandes varia-tions; il fait chaud durant presque toute l'année.

Un excellent réseau de communications —routes, voies ferrées, aéroport et port— place Valence à la tête des grandes villes espagnoles.

Les villes les plus importantes sont: Sagunto —très fameuse dans l'Antiquité—, Liria —centre musical de la province—, Cullera et Gandía —centres touristiques de grande importance—, Carcagente —grand centre producteur d'oranges—, Játiva, Sueca, Alcira, Requena, etc.

Le folklore est très brillant et se manifeste surtout lors des «fallas» qui ont lieu le jour de Saint Joseph. La ville déborde de vie et de gaieté au milieu des feux d'artifice et de la musique. Mention spéciale doit également être faite de la Foire de Juillet.

Valence, capitale de la province, a 583.151 habitants. C'est une ville charmante de caractère méditerranéen, gaie et lumineuse. Elle possède de grands monuments: le Palais du Marquis de Dos Aguas, La Lonja, El Miguelete, la Cathédrale, le Musée Provincial des Beaux-Arts, le Musée National de céramique «González Martí», le Musée Paléontologique et le Musée de la Préhistoire.

La région valencienne a donné à la cuisine espagnole son plat le plus connu dans le monde: la «paella», sorte de symphonie gastronomique sur le thème du riz.

VALENCIA, with an area of 10,763 sq. kms. and a population of 1,574,712, is one of the most prosperous provinces of the Spanish Levante or East Coast region. Essentially agricultural, it mainly produces rice and citrus fruits: indeed, the oranges of Valencia are known the world over. Where industry is concerned, Valencia has been able to adapt her traditional crafts to the needs of the times, and so produces excellent furniture, leather, silks, and ceramics of all types.

The most important industries are those of paper, cement and electric power production. There are steel mills at Sagunto and large shipyards and iron and steel industries in the port of Valencia.

The climate varies little throughout the year, warm temperatures being the rule for most of the year.

Valencia has a singularly good network of road rail, sea and air communications and heads all Spanish provinces in this respect.

The leadings towns are: Sagunto —famous even in remote times—, Liria —musical centre of the province—; Cullera and Gandía —very important tourist centres—; Carcagente —noted for its orange production—; Játiva, Sueca, Alcira, and Requena.

The brilliant folklore of the province finds its maximum expressions in the «fallas» on the feast of St. Joseph, which offer scenes of great rejoicing in which fireworks, music and good humour are blended. The July Fair is equally famous.

The city of Valencia, with its 583,151 inhabitants, is a lovely city on the Mediterranean with a gay and luminous air, Its most outstanding buildings from the artistic point of view are the Palacio del Marqués de Dos Aguas, the Lonja (exchange), the Miguelete tower, the Catedral, the Provincial Museum of Fine Arts, the «González Marti» National Museum of Ceramics and the Prehistoric and Paleontological Museums.

The region of Valencia has given Spanish cooking a dish known all over the world: «paella», which may without lear of exaggeration be described as a gastronomic symphony on a rice theme.

VALENCIA ist mit ihrer Ausdehnung von 10.763 km.² und ihren 1.574.712 Einwohnern eine der blühendsten und charakteristischsten Provinzen der spanischen Levante-Küste. Die Provinz ist hauptsächlich der Landwirtschaft gewidmet und produziert vor allem Reis sowie Apfelsinen und Zitronen. Die Apfelsinen der Provinz Valencia sind in der ganzen Welt bekannt. In industrieller Hinsicht hat Valencia es verstanden, ihr Kunsthandwerk der modernen Zeit anzupassen und hat die Herstellung ihrer typischen Prudukte wie Möbel, Leder, Keramik und Seiden vergrössert.

Die wichtigsten Industrien sind die Papier-und die Zement-Industrie sowie die Kraftwerke. Es gibt Hochöfen in Sagunto, grosse Schiffswerften im Hafen von Valencia und eine bedeutende Hüttenindustrie.

Das Klima weist keine grossen Gegensätze auf, und die Temperaturen sind während des grössten Teils des Jahres warm.

Infolge ihres ausgezeichneten Verbindungsnetzes —Landstrassen, Eisenbahnlinien, Flughafen und Seehafen— steht Valencia an der Spitze der spanischen Hauptstädte.

Bedeutende Ortschaften sind Sagunto —die bereits im Altertum berühmte Stadt—, Liria —musikalisches Zentrum der Provinz—, Cullera und Gandia —wichtige Touristenzentren—, Carcagente —entrum der Apfelsinenproduktion—, Játiva, Sueca, Alcira, Requena, usw.

Der reiche Volksbrauch findet seinen höchsten Ausdruck in den «Fallas» am Tage des San José: hier verbinden sich das Feuer, die Musik und die frohe Stimmung zu einem rauschenden Fest. Ebenso berühmt ist der Jahrmarkt im Monat Juli.

Die Hauptstadt ist mit ihren 583.151 Einwohnern eine schöne, lebensfrohe Stadt mit ausgeprägtem Mittelmeercharakter. Sie besitzt bedeutende Kunstdenkmäler, unter denen besonders der Palacio del Marqués de Dos Aguas, La Lonja, El Miguelete, die Kathedrale, das Provinzmuseum der Schö-

nen Künste, das Staatliche Keramikmuseum «González Martí» sowie das Paleontologische und das Prähistorische Museum hervorzuheben sind.

Das Gebiet von Valencia hat der spanischen Küche das in der Welt bekannteste Gericht geliefert: die «Paella», eine Art gastronomischer Symphonie über den Reis.

CONJUNTO MONUMENTAL

LONJA. Plaza del Mercado. Uno de los más interesantes monumentos del gótico civil de España, de finales del siglo XV.
Horas de visita: Laborables, de 9 a 13 y de 16 a 18. Verano, de 9 a 14 y de 17 a 20. Domingos, por la mañana.

PALACIO DE LA GENERALIDAD. Calle de Caballeros. Antiguo parlamento de la ciudad. Construcción de los siglos XV y XVI; estilo gótico mediterráneo.
Horas de visita: De 9 a 14 y de 16 a 19.

TORRES DE SERRANOS. Plaza de los Fueros. Puerta gótica de las antiguas murallas de la ciudad, finales del siglo XV.
Horas de visita: De 9 a 13 y de 16 a 18. Verano, de 9 a 14 y de 17 a 20.

CATEDRAL. Plaza de la Virgen, del Micalet y de la Almoina. Se comenzó a construir en la segunda mitad del siglo XIII. Diversos estilos. Destaca su puerta románica del Palau y la capilla del Santo Cáliz, interesante construcción gótica de mediados del siglo XIV.
Horas de visita: De 9 a 13 y de 15 a 18. Verano, de 9 a 13 y de 16 a 19.
Entrada al museo y tesoro: 10 ptas.

IGLESIA Y MUSEO DEL PATRIARCA. Calle de la Nave. Fundación del Patriarca y Virrey de Valencia San Juan de Ribera, siglos XVI y XVII. Magnífico claustro renacimiento. Su museo guarda obras de arte de gran valor, entre ellas varias de El Greco. Para visitarlas dirigirse al conserje.
Horas de visita: De 11 a 13 y de 17 a 19. Entrada al Museo: 10 pesetas.

NUESTRA SEÑORA DE LOS DESAMPARADOS. Plaza de la Virgen. Edificio del siglo XVII. Grandiosa cúpula pintada al fresco por Palomino.
Horas de visita: Las horas de culto.

MUSEO PROVINCIAL DE BELLAS ARTES. Calle de San Pío V. La mayor parte de sus fondos están constituidos por primitivos de la Escuela Valenciana. Se exhiben, además, obras de Juan de Juanes, Velázquez, Goya, etc.
Horas de visita: Todos los días de 10 a 14. Entrada: 10 pesetas.

MUSEO HISTORICO MUNICIPAL. Plaza del Caudillo. Ayuntamiento. Se exhiben interesantes recuerdos históricos de la ciudad y notables obras de arte.
Horas de visita: Laborables de 9 a 13.

MUSEO NACIONAL DE CERAMICA «GON-
ZALEZ MARTI». Rinconada de García Sánchez. Interesante y nutrida colección de
cerámica valenciana y de otras proceden-
cias, de diversas épocas y estilos.
Horas de visita: De 11 a 14 y de 17 a 20.
En verano, de 17 a 21.
Entrada: 10 pesetas.
MUSEO DE PREHISTORIA. Plaza de Manises.
De sumo interés para conocer las culturas
de la región. Reproducciones de pinturas
rupestres.
Horas de visita: Laborables, de 9 a 13.
MUSEO PALEONTOLOGICO. Calle del Al-
mudín. Instalado en un antiguo almacén
de granos del siglo XVI. Destacada colec-
ción de fósiles del cuaternario suramericano.
Horas de visita: Todos los días, de 10 a 13.
ARCHIVO GENERAL DEL REINO DE VA-
LENCIA. Plaza de Galicia.
Horas de visita: De 11,30 a 13,30.

ENSEMBLE MONUMENTAL

*LONJA. Place du Marché. Un des monu-
ments les plus intéressants du gothique
civil d'Espagne, de fin du XVᵉ siècle.*
Heures de visite: *Jours ouvrables, de 9 à
13 et de 16 à 18. Eté de 9 à 14 et de 17 à 20.
Dimanches matin.*
*PALAIS DE LA GENERALITE. Calle de Ca-
balleros. Ancien parlement de la ville. Construction des XV et XVIᵉ ss. Style gothique
méditerranéen.*
Heures de visite: *De 9 à 14 et de 16 à 19.*
*TORRES DE SERRANOS. Plaza de los Fueros.
Porte gothique des anciennes murailles de
la ville, fin du XVᵉ s.*
Heures de visite: *De 9 à 13 et de 16 à 18.
Eté: de 9 à 14 et de 17 à 20.*
*CATHEDRALE. Plaza de la Virgen, del Micalet
et de la Almoina. On commença —à la
construire dans la seconde moitié du XIIIᵉ s.
Divers styles. On remarque la porte romane
du Palau et la Chapelle du St. Calice, inté-
ressante construction gothique du milieu
du XIVᵉ.*
Heures de visite: *De 9 à 13 et de 15 à 18.
Eté de 9 à 13 et de 16 à 19.*
Entrée au musée et trésor: *10 ptas.*
*EGLISE ET MUSEE DU PATRIARCHE. Calle
de la Nave. Fondation du Patriarche et
Vice-Roi de Valence, St. Jean de Ribera,
XVI et XVIIᵉ. Magnifique cloitre renaissance.
Son musée garde des oeuvres d'art de
grande valeur parmi lesquelles plusieurs
du Gréco. Pour visiter, s'adresser au con-
cierge.*
Heures de visite: *De 11 à 13 et de 17 à 19.*
Entrée au Musée: *10 ptas.*
*NOTRE DAME DES DESEMPARES. Plaza
de la Virgen. Edifice du XVIIᵉ. Grandiose
coupole peinte à la fresque par Palomino.*
Heures de visite: *Les heures de culte.*

*MUSEE PROVINCIAL DES BEAUX- ARTS.
Calle de San Pío V. La plupart de ses fonds
sont constitués par des primitifs de l'Ecole
Valencienne. Il contient en outre des oeuvres de Juan de Juanes, Velázquez, Goya,
etcetera.*
Heures de visite: *Tous les jours de 10 à 14.*
Entrée: *10 ptas.*
*MUSEE HISTORIQUE MUNICIPAL. Plaza
del Caudillo. Hôtel de Ville. On y montre
d'intéressants souvenirs historiques de la
ville et de remarquables oeuvres d'art.*
Heures de visite: *Jours ouvrables de 9 à 13.*
*MUSEE NATIONAL DE CERAMIQUE «GON-
ZALEZ MARTI». Intéressante et abondante
collection de céramique de Valence et
d'autres provenances de divers styles et
époques. Se trouve au coin de García
Sánchez.*
Heures de visita: *De 11 à 14 et de 17 à 20.
En été: de 17 à 21.*
Entrée: *10 ptas.*
*MUSEE DE PREHISTOIRE. Plaza de Manises.
De grand intérêt pour connaître les cultures
de la région. Reproduction de peintures ru-
pestres.*
Heures de visite: *Jours ouvrables de 9 à 13.*
*MUSEE PALEONTOLOGIQUE. Calle del Al-
mudín. Installé dans un ancien magasin
de grains du XVIᵉ s. Remarquable collection
de fossiles du quaternaire sudaméricain.*
Heures de visite: *Tous les jours de 10 à 13.*
*ARCHIVES GENERALES DU ROYAUME DE
VALENCE. Plaza de Galicia.*
Heures de visite: *De 11,30 à 13,30.*

MONUMENTS

EXCHANGE. Market Square. One of the
most interesting civil Gothic monuments
in Spain, built at the end of 15th century.
Visiting hours: Working days from 9 to 13
and from 16 to 18.
Summer from 9 to 14 and from 17 to 20.
Sundays in the morning.
PALACE OF THE «GENERALIDAD». Calle
de los Caballeros. Former city parliament.
15th and 16th century construction. Mediterranean Gothic style.
Visiting hours: From 9 to 14 and from 16
to 19.
TORRES DE SERRANOS. Plaza de los Fueros.
Gothic gateway in the old city walls, end
of 15th century.
Visiting hours: From 9 to 13 and from 16
to 18. Summer from 9 to 14 and from 17
to 20.
CATHEDRAL. In the Plazas Virgen, Micalet
and Almoina. Construction was begun
during second half of the 13th century.
Various styles. Note the romanic Palau
door and the Holy Chalice chapel, interesting Gothic construction of middle of 14th
century.

Visiting hours: From 9 to 13 and from 15 to 18. Summer, 9 to 13 and from 16 to 19. Entrance to Museum and Treasury: 10 ptas.

CHURCH AND PATRIARCH MUSEUM. Calle de la Nave. Founded by the Patriarch and Viceroy of Valencia, San Juan de Ribera, 16th and 17th centuries. Magnificent renaissance cloister. The museum houses works of art of great value, including several El Greco. Contact concierge for visits.
Visiting hours: From 11 to 13 and from 17 to 19.
Entrance to Museum: 10 ptas.

NUESTRA SEÑORA DE LOS DESAMPARADOS (Our Lady of the Helpless). Plaza de la Virgen. 17th century building. Magnificent cupola, al fresco painted by Palomino.
Visiting hours: Hours of worship.

FINE ARTS PROVINCIAL MUSEUM. Calle de San Pío V. The majority of exhibits are by primitive artists of the Valencian School. Works by Juan de Juanes, Velázquez, Goya, etc., are alsoe, exhibited.
Visiting hours: Everyday from 10 to 14.
Entrance: 10 ptas.

MUNICIPAL HISTORICAL MUSEUM. Plaza del Caudillo. Town Hall. Interesting historical remains of the city and notable works of art are exhibited.
Visiting hours: Working days from 9 to 13.

GONZALEZ MARTI NATIONAL CERAMICS MUSEUM. Rinconada de García Sánchez. Interesting, varied collection of Valencian ceramics and also from other sources, of different periods and styles.
Visiting hours: From 11 to 14 and from 17 to 20.
In summer from 17 to 21.
Entrance: 10 ptas.

PREHISTORIC MUSEUM. Plaza de Manises. Most interesting for learning about cultures of the region. Reproductions of Rupestrian paintings.
Visiting hours: Working days, from 9 to 13.

PALEONTHOLOGICAL MUSEUM. Calle del Almudín. Installed in a former granary of the 16th century. Noteworthy collection of fossils of the South American Quaternary.
Visiting hours: Everyday from 10 to 13.

GENERAL ARCHIVES OF THE KINGDOM OF VALENCIA. Plaza de Galicia.
Visiting hours: From 11,30 to 13,30.

SEHENSWÜRDIGKEITEN

LONJA. Plaza del Mercado. Eines der interessantesten Monumente der zivilen gotischen Baukunst in Spanien. Es stammt aus dem XV. Jahrhundert.
Besichtigungszeiten: Werktags 9,00 - 13,00 und 16,00 - 18,00 Uhr. Sommer: 9,00 - 14,00 und 17,00 - 20,00 Uhr. Sonntags: Nur vormittags.

PALACIO DE LA GENERALIDAD. Calle de Caballeros. Altes Parlament der Stadt. Bauwerk aus dem XV/XVI. Jahrh.; mittelländischer gotischer Stil.
Besichtigungszeiten: 9,00 - 14,00 und 16,00 - 19,00 Uhr.

TORRES DE SERRANOS (Serrano-Türme). Plaza de los Fueros. Gotisches Tor der alten Stadtmauer aus dem XV. Jahrh.
Besichtigungszeiten: 9,00 - 13,00 und 16,00 - 18,00 Uhr. Sommer: 9,00 - 14,00 und 17,00 - 20,00 Uhr.

KATHEDRALE. Plaza de la Virgen, del Micalet und de la Almoina. Mit den Bauarbeiten wurde im XIII. Jahrh. Begonnen. Verschiedenartige Stile. Hervorstechen ihre romanische Tür, genannt Puerta del Palau und ihre Capilla del Santo Cáliz gotischen Stils aus der Mitte des XIVJahrh.
Besichtigungszeiten: 9,00 - 13,00 und 15,00 - 18,00 Uhr. Sommer: 9,00 - 13,00 und 16,00 - 19,00 Uhr.
Besichtigung des Museums und der Schatzkammer: 10 peseten.

KIRCHE UND MUSEUM DEL PATRIARCA. Calle de la Nave. Gründung des Patriarchen und Vizekönigs von Valencia St. Johannes von Rivera aus dem XVI/XVII. Jahrh. Prächtiger Renaissance- Kreuzgang. Das Museum bewahrt kostbare Kunstwerke, unter ihnen verschiedene von El Greco, auf. Auf Wunsch zeigt der Pförtner diese Gemälde.
Besichtigungszeiten: 11,00 - 13,00 und 17,00 - 19,00 Uhr.
Eintritt in das Museum: 10 peseten.

BASILICA NUESTRA SEÑORA DE LOS DESAMPARADOS. Plaza de la Virgen. Gabäude aus dem XVII. Jahrh. Kuppel mit grossartigen Freskomalereien von Palomino.
Besichtigungszeiten: Während der Gottesdienste.

LANDESMUSEUM DER SCHONEN KÜNSTE. Strasse San Pío V. Der grösste Teil des Reichtums dieses Museums besteht aus Kunstwerken der Maler des XIV/XV. Jahrh. aus der valencianischen Schule. Ausserdem werden Gemälde von Juan de Juanes, Velazquez, Goya usw, ausgestellt.
Besichtigungszeiten: Täglich von 10,00 - 14,00 Uhr.
Eintritt: 10 peseten.

STADTISCHES GESCHICHTSMUSEUM. Plaza del Caudillo, Rathaus. Es können interessante historische Andenken der Stadt sowie bemerkenswerte Kunstwerke besichtigt werden.
Besichtigungszeiten: Werktags: 9,00 - 13,00 Uhr.

NATIONALES KERAMIK MUSEUM «GONZALEZ MARTI». Rinconada de García Sánchez, interessante und reichhaltige Keramik-Sammlung aus Valencia und anderer Herkunft, die verschiedene Epochen und Stile umfasst.

Besichtigungszeiten: *11,00 - 14,00 und 17,00 - 20,00 Uhr.*
Sommer: *17,00 - 21,00 Uhr.*
Eintritt: *10 peseten.*
PRAHISTORISCHES MUSEUM. *Plaza de Manises. Sehr interessant, um die Kulturen dieses Gebietes kennenzulernen. Reproduktionen von Felsmalereien.*
Besichtigungszeiten: *Werktags: 9,00 - 13,00 Uhr.*
PALAONTOLOGISCHES MUSEUM. *Calle del Almudin. Befindet sich in einem alten Getreidelagerhaus aus dem XVI. Jahrh. Wertvolle Fossilien-Sammlung aus dem südamerikanischen Quartär.*
Besichtigungszeiten: *Täglich von 10,00 - 13,00 Uhr.*
GENERALARCHIV DES KONIGREICHS VALENCIA. *Plaza de Galicia.*
Besichtigungszeiten: *11,30 - 13,30 Uhr.*

HOTELES—HÔTELS—HOTELS—HOTELS HOSTALES—HÔTELLERIE— HOSTELRIES—GASTHÄUSER PENSIONES—PENSIONS—BOARDING- HOUSES—PENSIONEN

Valencia

ALHAMBRA. Convento San Francisco, 2. Telf. 21 72 50. H ****.
ASTORIA PALACE. Rodrigo Botel, 5. Telf. 28 95 90. H ****.
INGLES. Marqués de Dos Aguas, 6. Telf. 21 45 53. H ***.
EXCELSIOR. Hermanas Chabás, 5. Telf. 21 30 40. H ***.
LLAR. Colón, 46. Telf. 22 72 94. H ***.
OLTRA. Cotanda, 4. Telf. 22 31 90.
REINA VICTORIA. Barcas, 4 y 6. Telf. 21 13 60. H ***.
ROYAL. Pintor Sorolla, 21. Telf. 21 31 21. H ***.
BRISTOL. Abadía San Martín, 3. Telf. 22 48 95.
LA MARCELINA. Avda. Neptuno, 76. Telf. 23 08 67. H **.
METROPOL. Játiva, 23. Telf. 21 44 83. H **.
SOROLLA. Convento Santa Clara, 5. Telf. 22 32 23. H **.
ALCAZAR. Mosén Femades, 11. Telf. 21 46 32. H *.
CONTINENTAL. Correos, 8. Telf. 21 72 18. H *.
EUROPA. Ribera, 4. Telf. 22 05 87. H *.
INTERNACIONAL. Bailén, 8. Telf. 21 45 65. H *.
LAURIA-ROMA. Roger de Lauria, 4. Telf. 22 34 90. H *.
LES MARINES. Avda. Neptuno, 14. Telf. 23 28 47. H *.
LA PEPICA. Avda. de Neptuno, 2. Telf. 23 17 85. H *.
LONDRES. Hermanas Chabás, 1. Telf. 22 00 90. H ***.
AMERICA. Sangre, 9, 6.º. Telf. 22 38 83. P **.

AVENIDA. Caudillo, 2. Telf. 21 31 82. HR **.
BORDONADO. Marqués de Campo, 10. Telf. 37 09 58. HR **.
CHICOTE. Avda. Neptuno, 37. Telf. 23 45 41. H **.
FLORIDA. Padilla, 4. Telf. 21 30 35. HR **.
GRAN VIA. Gran Via Marqués del Turia, 46, 1.º. Telf. 27 06 37. H **.
LIFRAN. Mariano Benlliure, 9, 2.º. Telf. 22 68 11. H **.
MEDITERRANEO. Grabador Selma, 5, 1.º y 2.º. Telf. 21 15 42. H **.
MIRAMAR. Avda. de Neptuno, 34. Telf. 23 65 81. HR **.
MIRIAM. Plaza Nazaret (La Punta). Telf. 23 14 64. H **.
MUNICH. Paz, 2. Telf. 21 18 22. H **.
NORTE. Ntra. Sra. de Gracia, 8. Telf. 21 31 40. HR **.
ORIENTE. Plaza del Caudillo, 9. Telf. 22 12 90. H **.
PANAMERICA. Caudillo, 13, 7.º. Telf. 22 24 71. HR **.
RIALTO. Caudillo, 9. Telf. 22 17 90. H **.
VALENCIA. Convento San Francisco, 7. Telf. 21 72 94. H **.
LAS VEGAS. Plaza Nazaret-La Punta, s/n., 1.º. Telf. 23 09 90. H **.
VENECIA. En Llop, 5. Telf. 21 73 12. H **.
LA ALCOYANA. Bailén, 6. Telf. 21 41 55. H *.
ALICANTE. Ribera, 8, 2.º. Telf. 21 82 53. H *.
ALMINAR. Moratín, 15, 3.º. Telf. 21 69 20. P *.
APARICIO. Torno del Hospital, 3, 1.º, 2.º y 3.º. Telf. 31 52 80. HR *.
ARAGON. Avda. del Puerto, 26. Telf. 27 18 46. P *.
AYORA. Pérez Pujol, 4, 2.º. Telf. 21 03 91. P *.
LA BARRACA. Avda. Neptuno, 38, 1.º. Telf. 23 39 95. HR *.
CARRASCO. Buenos Aires, 6, 1.º. Telf. 27 71 16. HR *.
CASA BLAYET. Ctra. Nazaret-Oliva, 19. H *.
CASTELAR. Ribera, 1, 3.º. Telf. 21 55 92. HR *.
COLON. Isabel de Villena, 21. Telf. 23 03 62. P *.
LA CONQUENSE. Pelayo, 50, 1.º. Telf. 21 88 90. P *.
DOS PUERTAS. Mesón de Teruel, 4. Telf. 22 13 95. HR *.
ESLAVA. Calvo Sotelo, 26. Telf. 21 47 52. H *.
ESPAÑA. Embajador Vich, 5, 2.º. Telf. 22 97 39. HR *.
ESTE. Avda. Barón de Cárcer, 37, 2.º. Telf. 22 22 47. H *.
LA FEDERACION. Nave, 7, 1.º y 4.º. Telf. 21 06 85. H *.
HOSPEDERIA DEL PILAR. Mercado, 19. Telf. 22 02 94. H *.
HOSPEDERIA SAN ANDRES. Matemático Marzal, 3, bajo, 1.º, 2.º y 3.º. Telf. 22 97 55. HR *.

KROKO. Bailén, 28, 5.º. Telf. 21 47 69. ⋈R *.
MADRID. Avda. Neptuno, 58. Telf. 23 23 87.
⋈ *.
MORATIN. Moratín, 15, 5.º. Telf. 22 12 20.
P *.
EL PARLAMENTO. Transits, 5. Telf. 21 92 38.
⋈R **.
LA PAZ. Avda. Neptuno, 72. Telf. 23 22 40.
⋈R **.
PORT-MAR. Avda. Doncel Luis Felipe García
Sanchiz, 336, 2.º, 3.º y 4.º. ⋈R *.
PUERTO. J. J. Sister, 6, 1.º y 3.º. Telf. 22 33 76.
P *.
EL RINCON. Carda, 11. Telf. 21 05 83. ⋈R *.
SAN ROMO. Arzobispo Mayoral, 5. Telf.
21 34 00. ⋈R *.
SAN VICENTE. San Vicente, 57, 2.º. Telf.
21 52 64. ⋈ *.
EL SOL. Avda. Neptuno, 60. Telf. 23 23 94.
⋈R *.
TERMINUS. Bailén, 18, 1.º. Telf. 21 36 84.
⋈R *.
UNIVERSAL. Baseas, 5. Telf. 21 07 85. ⋈ *.
VENTA DEL MAR. Ctra. Punta del Mar
(Nazaret), 89, 1.º. Telf. 23 01 48. ⋈R *.
VILLA AMPARITO. Avda. Neptuno, 40, 1.º.
Telf. 23 23 81. ⋈R *.
YUKUAMA. Pelayo, 7, 1.º. Telf. 22 30 34. ⋈R *.

Alcira

MORTES. Mayor San Agustín, 11. Telf.
80 30 02. ⋈ *.

Alcudia de Carlet

CASA GALBIS. Antonio Almela, 15. Telf.
282. ⋈R *.

Barig

MONTE MONDUBER. Ptda. de la Droba-
Rita Mondúber. Telf. 17. H **.

Bellús

BALNEARIO DE BELLUS. Emp. Ctra. Va-
lencia-Alcoy a Benicasim. Telf. 15. ⋈ *.

Carcagente

ESPAÑA. Cabo Lloret, 2. Telf. 230. P *.

Cofrentes

BALNEARIO HERVIDEROS DE COFRENTES.
Afueras. Telf. 1. H **.

Cuartell

LOS VALLES. Ctra. Valencia-Barcelona, kiló-
metro 30. Telf. 114 de Faura. H *.

Cullera

SICANIA. Ctra. el Faro, s/n. Telf. 223. H ***.
MAR Y SOL. Faro de Cullera, s/n. Telf. 281. H *.
SAFI. Faro de Cullera-Ptda. del Dosel. Telf.
542. H *.

EL CID. Plaza del Dosel. ⋈R *.
LAMA. Cabañas, 4, 8.º. Telf. 815. ⋈ *.
LA PAZ. Alcázar de Toledo, 39, 2.º. Telf.
563. ⋈R *.
EL SIGLO. Maestro Valls, 1. Telf. 9. ⋈ *.
LA TORRE. Valencia, 1, bajo y 4.º. Telf. 222.
⋈R *.

Chiva

LOMA DEL CASTILLO. Ctra. Madrid-Valencia, 320. Telf. 29. ⋈ **.

Chulilla

BALNEARIO DE CHULILLA. Afueras de Chulilla (Fuencaliente). Telf. 13. ⋈ *.

Daimuz

OLIMPICO. El Pedregal. ⋈R *.

Gandía

BAYREN I. Paseo de Neptuno, s/n. Telf.
91. H ***.
BAYREN II. Mallorca (playa), s/n. Telf. 117.
HR ***.
SAFARI. Continuación calle Canarias, s/n.
Telf. 120. H ***.
SAN LUIS. Paseo de Neptuno, 6. Telf. 238.
H ***.
EUROPA. Levante, 12. Telf. 96. H *.
DUCAL MESON. Santo Duque, 7, 2.º y 3.º.
Telf. 87 27 27. ⋈R **.
ERNESTO. Valencia, 40. Telf. 87 10 00. ⋈ **.
REXY. Mayor, 48. Telf. 87 11 51. ⋈ **.
TRITON. Iglesia, 2, 2.º y 3.º. Telf. 389 del
Grao. ⋈R **.
VICTORIA. Plaza del Marqués de Campo, 9.
Telf. 87 12 00. ⋈ **.
FIN DE SEMANA. Mare Nostrum, 35, 1.º y
2.º. Telf. 97. ⋈ *.
LA VELLA. José Antonio, 23. Telf. 1790. ⋈R *.

Játiva

MORENO. San Francisco, 36. Telf. 88 30 31.
P *.

Oliva

PAUPI. Roger de Lauria, 2. Telf. 202. ⋈ *.
PEIRO. General Aranda, 26, bajo y 2.º. Telf.
436. P *.

Paterna

NITRE. Pérez Galdós, 6, bajo. P *.

Perelló (El) (Sueca)

ANTINA. Buenavista, 4. Telf. 27. H **.
NICOLA. Buenavista, 5. Telf. 26. P *.

Perellonet (El) (Valencia)

RECATI. El Perellonet. Ctra. Valencia-Oliva,
km. 18. Telf. 23 38 25. H ***.

Piles

GLORIA MAR. Playa. ⊞ *.

Puerto (El) (Sagunto)

BAR TEIDE. Avda. José Antonio, 71. Telf. 86. ⊞ *.
EBRO. Avda. de la Hispanidad, 6, 2.º y 3.º. Telf. 508. ⊞R *.
EUROPA. Virgen del Carmen, 22 y 24, 1.º. Telf. 397. ⊞ *.

Puir de Santa María (El)

BORJA. Progreso, 35, bajo. Telf. 71. ⊞R *.

Puzol

MONTE PICAYO. Paraje denominado Monte Picayo. Telf. 25 31 59. H *****.

Requena

BALNEARIO FUENTE PODRIDA. Ctra. Nal. 322. Telf. 6. H *.
SOL. Ctra. Nal. 3, km. 281. ⊞R **.

Sagunto

LA PINADA. Ctra. Nal. Sagunto-Burgos, 3, bajo y 1.º. Telf. 572. ⊞R *.

Saler (El) (Valencia)

PARADOR NACIONAL LUIS VIVES. Paral. Telf. 23 68 50. H ****.

Serra

LES FORQUES. Puntal de Les Forqués, s/n. Telf. 2. H *.

Sueca

ARIANE. Plaza Mareny de Vilches. H *.
MARI. Avda. Caudillo, 75. Telf. 208. P *.

Tabernes Blanques

ESTELA. Avda. Franco, 128. Telf. 145. ⊞ **.

Tabernes de Valldigna

ERNESTO. Primo de Rivera, 46. Telf. 765. P *.
VILA URSULA. Playa. ⊞R *.

Torrente

GRAN HOTEL LIDO. Vedat de Torrene. Urb. Sta. Apolonia. Telf. 55 15 00. H ***.

Utiel

LA ABUELA. Ctra. Madrid-Valencia, 270. Telf. 375. ⊞R **.
POTAJERO CHICO. Ctra. Madrid-Valencia, 271. Telf. 287. ⊞R **.

APARTAMENTOS TURISTICOS
APPARTEMENTS TOURISTIQUES
TOURIST APARTMENTS
APARTEMENTHÄUSER

Canet de Berenguer

CANET. Playa Canet de Berenguer. 2.ª C.

Cullera

ANA. Avda. Alicante, s/n. 3.ª C.
CASA RITA. El Dosel de San Lorenzo, s/n. 2.ª C.
EDIFICIO HOLANDA. Cabañal s/n.
ELCKER. Partida Dosel de San Lorenzo. 2.ª C.
ESPAÑA. Particular. 3.ª C.
FRANCIA. Cabañal s/n. 3.ª C.
EL GALEON. Plaza Mongrell, s/n. 1.ª C.
HINTZF. Partida Dosel de San Lorenzo. 2.ª C.
MARCH. Homero, s/n. 3.ª C.
OASIS. Plaza de la Victoria, s/n. 3.ª C.
PIONER. Plaza de la Victoria, s/n. 3.ª C.
LA PONDEROSA. 18 de Julio, s/n. 3.ª C.
EL RACO. Paraje La Magnolia, s/n. 3.ª C.
EL RACO. Frente a Santa Marta. 3.ª C.
LA RADA. Marqués de la Romana, s/n. 2.ª y 3.ª C.
SANTA MARTA. Santa Marta. 3.ª C.

Gandía

EL ALAMO. Del Atlántico, s/n. 3.ª C.
ALBAR. Trav. Atlántico-Playa de Gandía.
ALFARO. Trav. Atlántico-Playa de Gandía. 3.ª C.
ALFONSO. Playa de Gandía. 2.ª C.
ALMOINES. Playa de Gandía. 2.ª C.
ANCORA. Trav. Alcoy-Playa de Gandía. 3.ª C.
LAS ARENAS. Paseo Neptuno-Playa de Gandía. 3.ª C.
BIARRITZ. Atlántico, 22-Playa de Gandía. 3.ª C.
BONANZA. Mare Nostrum, 83-Playa de Gandía. 3.ª C.
BRISA. Paseo de Neptuno, 30. 1.ª C.
BRISA. Paseo Marítimo, s/n. 3.ª C.
BUANA. Cibeles. 3.ª C.
CALIFORNIA. Calle 25-Playa de Gandía. 3.ª C.
CAPRI. Paseo de Neptuno, 68. 3.ª C.
CLIBOMAR. Clibomar. 1.ª C.
COLONIA DUCAL. Colonia Ducal-Bloque E. Playa de Gandía. 3.ª C.
COLONIA DUCAL. Colonia Ducal-Bloque C. 2.ª C.
COLONIA DUCAL. Colonia Ducal-Bloque E. 2.ª C.
COLLADO. Colonia Ducal-Playa de Gandía. 3.ª C.
COSTA BLANCA. Paseo de Neptuno, s/n. 3.ª C.
CHAPER. Cibeles-Playa de Gandía. 3.ª C.
CHERMIL. Atlántico, s/n. 3.ª C.
CHERMIL. Mare Nostrum-Playa de Gandía. 3.ª C.
CHOPERA. Mallorca-Playa de Gandía. 3.ª C.

CHOVA. Atlántico, s/n. 3.ª C.
DANDY. Calle 20-Playa de Gandía. 3.ª C.
DELFIN. Mallorca, s/n.-Playa de Gandía. 2.ª C.
DELFIN. Mallorca-Playa de Gandía. 3.ª C.
DEUSA. Atlántico-Playa de Gandía. 3.ª C.
DUCAL. Colonia Ducal-Playa de Gandía. 2.ª y 3.ª C.
EDIFICIO LANGAY. Calle 30 del Plano, s/n. 2.ª C.
ESTRELLA DE MAR. Mare Nostrum, 3-Playa de Gandía. 3.ª C.
FINITA. Mallorca-Playa de Gandía. 2.ª C.
GARCIA. Paseo de Neptuno, 17-Playa de Gandía.
GIRASOL. Mare Nostrum, s/n.-Playa de Gandía. 2.ª C.
LIBELULA. Calle 20-Playa de Gandía. 2.ª C.
MADRID. Calle, 16-Playa de Gandía. 2.ª y 3.ª C.
MALLORCA. Mallorca, s/n. 3.ª C.
MAÑO FERNANDEZ. Mare Nostrum, s/n. 3.ª C.
MAÑO VALLS. Mare Nostrum, 18. 3.ª C.
MARBELL. Paseo Neptuno, 36. 3.ª C.
MARBLAU. Paseo Neptuno, 54. 3.ª C.
MARI LOLA. Atlántico, 21-Playa de Gandía. 2.ª C.
MARTI. Atlántico, 24-Playa de Gandía. 3.ª C.
MARTIN. Paseo Neptuno-Playa de Gandía. 3.ª C.
MEDITERRANEO. Mallorca, s/n.-Playa de Gandía. 3.ª C.
MIÑANA. Atlántico-Playa de Gandía. 3.ª C.
EL MOLINO. Paseo de Neptuno, 6. 3.ª C.
MOLTO. Cibeles-Playa de Gandía. 3.ª C.
MONACO. Baleares-Playa de Gandía. 3.ª C.
MONTECARLO. Av. de la Paz, 30. 3.ª C.
MOREMAR. Mallorca-Playa de Gandía. 3.ª C.
NEPTUNO. Paseo Neptuno, 10-Playa de Gandía. 1.ª C.
NIZA. Mallorca. 3.ª C.
PEREZ. Paseo Neptuno, s/n.-Playa de Gandía. 3.ª C.
RIBES. Paseo Neptuno, s/n.-Playa de Gandía. 3.ª C.
ROMERO. Paseo Neptuno, s/n.-Playa de Gandía. 3.ª C.
ROMPEOLAS. Mare Nostrum, s/n.-Playa de Gandía. 3.ª C.
ROSAMAR. Calle 30, s/n.-Playa de Gandía. 2.ª y 3.ª C.
SANFELIX. Atlántico, s/n.-Playa de Gandía. 3.ª C.
SAN REMO. Mare Nostrum, s/n.-Playa de Gandía. 3.ª C.
SOL-MAR. Mallorca, s/n. 3.ª C.
EL TIMON. Atlántico, s/n. 1.ª C.
TOBA. Mallorca, s/n. 2.ª C.
TORMO. Atlántico, s/n.-Playa de Gandía. 3.ª C.
TRITON. Mare Nostrum, s/n.-Playa de Gandía. 3.ª C.
VILA. Colonia Ducal-Playa de Gandía.
VILLA AMPARO. Mare Nostrum-Playa de Gandía. 2.ª C.
VILLA CONCHITA. Mare Nostrum, 11-Playa de Gandía. 3.ª C.
VILLA FERNANDO. Mare Nostrum-Playa de Gandía. 2.ª C.
VILLA GREGORI. C/. Mallorca, s/n. Playa de Gandía. 3.ª C.
VILLA MARUJIN. Travesía Escrivá, s/n.-Playa de Gandía. 2.ª C.
VILLA MONICA. Mare Nostrum, s/n.-Playa de Gandía. 2.ª C.

El Perelló

MATOSES. Calle de las Américas, 26. 3.ª C.

Perellonet

ALBUJAIRA. Calle en proyecto. 3.ª C.

Piles

VILLA CERVANTES. Avda. del Mar, s/n. 3.ª C.

Sagunto

BAR PLAYA. General Mola, 103. 2.ª C.
CORINTO. Playa Almardá-Corinto. 3.ª C.
MON-TIBERIO. Camping Mon-Tiberio. 3.ª C.
LA PINADA. Carretera Sagunto-Burgos, km. 3. 2.ª C.

El Saler

ALFARO. Embarcadero, 5. 3.ª C.
COLLADO. Historiador Bori, 3. 3.ª C.
DASI. Embarcadero, 5. 3.ª C.
FORTEA. Embarcadero, 5. 3.ª C.
NAVARRO. Embarcadero, 6. 3.ª C.
PASTILLA. Aguilera, 3. 3.ª C.
RICART. Aguilera, 7. 3.ª C.

ACAMPAMIENTOS TURISTICOS
CAMPINGS
CAMPING SITES
ZELTPLÄTZE

VALENCIA. «Casa Alfonso». Km. 18 C.ª. Valencia-Alicante, por la costa 2.ª C.
VALENCIA. «El Saler». Km. 8 C.ª. Nazaret-Oliva. 1.ª C.
CULLERA. «Santa Marta». Km. 2 C.ª. Cullera al faro. 1.ª C.
GANDIA. «Gandía». Km. 7 C.ª. Valencia-Murcia. 2.ª C.
GANDIA. «Ros». Km. 70 C.ª. Valencia-Gandía. 2.ª C.
JARACO. «San Vicente». Km. 58 Ctra. Valencia-Alicante. 3.ª C.
JARACO. «Sol Mar». Ctra. Valencia-Almería. 3.ª C.
JERESA-GANDIA. «Caudelí». Km. 200 Ctra. Valencia-Murcia. 1.ª C.
OLIVA. «Euro Camping». Km. 190 Ctra. Valencia-Almería, por Gata. 2.ª C.
OLIVA. «Kiko». Km. 191 Ctra. Valencia-Alicante. 2.ª C.

OLIVA. «Olé». Km. 181,500 Ctra. Murcia-Valencia. 1.ª C.
OLIVA. «Pepe». Km. 177 Ctra. Almería-Valencia. s/c.
OLIVA. «Río Mar». A 500 metros Ctra. Valencia-Murcia. 3.ª C.
OLIVA. «San Fernando». Km. 80 Ctra. Valencia-Almería. 1.ª C.
OLIVA. «Sol». Km. 2 Ctra. Valencia-Murcia. 3.ª C.
SAGUNTO. «Mont-Tiberio». Km. 26 Ctra. Valencia-Barcelona. 2.ª C.

RESTAURANTES—RESTAURANTS
RESTAURANTS—RESTAURANTS

Valencia

VIVEROS. Jardines del Real, s/n.
LAS ARENAS. Playa de Levante, 52-64.
LES GRAELLES. Pl. de Galicia, s/n.
MARISQUERO. Félix Pizcueta, 7.
REAL CLUB NAUTICO. Paseo de Caro, s/n.
SOL Y SOMBRA. Don Juan de Austria, 7.
VILLUMA. Falangista Esteva, 4.
CAPRI, S. L. Muñoz Degrain, 1.
LA MARCELINA. Avda. Neptuno, 10.
MESON DEL CONDE. José Iturbi, 18.
LA PEPICA. Playa de Levante, 8.
LA PIZZERIA. Conde de Altea, 46.
TRES CEPAS. Playa de Levante, 24.
WAL-GUI. Avda. de Suecia, 15.
AVELINO. Avda. Pérez Galdós, 70.
LA BARRACA. Playa de Levante, 38
BENIMAR. Escuela de Deportes de la Iglesia.
CASA BALAGUER. Avda. Ramiro Ledesma, 210 bajo.
CASA CLEMENCIA. Avda. Primado Reig, 201.
CASA GIMENEZ. Pintor Domingo, 45.
CASA HONORIO. A. Cadarso, 23.
CASA NAVARRO. Pelayo, 9.
CASA OLANO. General San Martín, 13.
CASA PACO. Marcelina, 20.
CESAREO. Guillén de Castro, 15.
EL CID. Erudito Orellana, 10.
LOS CLAVELES. San Vicente, 98.
CHE TABERNA VASCA. Avda. José Antonio, 9.
CHICOTE. Playa de Levante, 36.
CHIMO. Playa de Levante, 38.
DOS PUERTAS. Mesón de Teruel, 4.
ESTACION NORTE. Játiva, s/n.
ESTIMAT. Playa de Levante, 18.
FAEMA. Pelayo, 6.
GARROFA. Camino Canal (frente 128).
GENARO. Avda. Neptuno, 48.
GOL. Eugenia Viñes, 1.
LA GRAN PAELLA. Burriana, 6.
GRAN RONDA. Pérez Galdós, 117.
GURE ETXEA. Almirante Cadarso, 6.
HOGAR GANADERO. Convento Santa Clara, 11.
JOCKEY. Embajador Vich, 20.
JUANET. Playa de Levante, 44.
LA LUNA. San Vicente, 57.

MESON DEL CAMPEADOR. San José de Calasanz, 28.
MIGUEL. Conde de Tremor, 12.
MIRAMAR. P. de Neptuno, 34.
MONKILI. Playa de Levante, 54.
NAVARRO. Arzobispo Mayoral, 5.
EL NIDO. Gran Vía Marqués del Turia, 78.
NORTE. Ntra. Sra. de Gracia, 8.
LA NUEVA TORERA. Colón, 1.
PACHI. Avda. Pérez Galdós, 60.
EL PAELLER. Julio Antonio, 17.
PALACE FESOL. Hernán Cortés, 7.
PALMERA. Avda. de los Mártires, 6.
PANAMA. Salamanca, 13.
LA PAZ. Avda. Neptuno, 72.
LOS PEDRALVINOS. Cura Femania, 8.
PEGASO. Cuenca, 2.
PERELLONET. Ctra. Nazaret-Oliva, 23.
RIBERA. Ribera, 9.
ROMERAL. Gran Vía Marqués del Turia, 62.
LA ROSA. Playa de Levante, 74.
EL SOL. Playa de Levante, 60.
TALENS. Matemático Marzal, 25.
LAS TINAJAS DE BUÑOL. Cirilo Amorós, 25.
TONI KEY. Cádiz, 27.
TRES CEPAS. Avda. del Puerto, 314-B.
UNIC. Cuenca, 21.
VANTA DE MONTIEL. Cádiz, 12.
VILLA AMPARITO. Playa Levante, 40.
ALCOYANAS BODEGAS. Triador, 27.
ARI. Molinell, 17.
AVENIDA. Avda. Burjasot, 245.
BALAGUER. Torno del Hospital, 13.
BELTRAN. Conde de Montornes, 28.
BODEGA. Cardenal Benlloch, 36.
BODEGON. Avda. del Doncel García Sanchis, 14.
BODEGON. CASA MIGUEL. Conde Montornes, 26.
EL BODEGON ESPAÑOL. Julio Antonio, 18.
BOQUERON DE PLATA. Torno Hospital, 1.
EL BOSQUE. Pelayo, 8.
CANO. Avda. del Puerto, 266.
CASA BOTELLA. Pelayo, 38.
CASA CARLOS. Avda. Cardenal Benlloch, 68.
CASA CARMELA. Isabel de Villena, 153.
CASA CERVERA. Borrul, 7.
CASA CONRADO. Virgen del Puig, 28.
CASA CORONAS. San Pío V, 4.
CASA ELIAS. Luis Oliag, 6.
CASA LORENZO. Pintor S. Abril, 42.
CASA MARCO. Alcañiz, 4.
CASA MEDINA. Denia, 53.
CASA PACO. Padre Jofre, 16.
CASA PEROL. Ercilla, 20.
CASA SILVERIO. Luis Oliag, 53.
CASA TALON. Camino Real de Madrid, 430.
CASA TONI. Pelayo, 22.
CASA VICENTE. Avda. Puerto, 144.
CIBELES. Viana, 9.
EL CISNE. Maestro Bellver, 46 bajo.
CIUDAD FALLERA. Primera calle en proyecto, 22.
COMIDAS ECONOMICAS. Pintor Domingo, 12.

COMIDAS ESMA. Zurradores, 5.
COMIDAS GIL. Nave, 20.
COMIDAS EL JEREZANO. Maldonado, 19 bajo.
COMIDAS EL MARQUESADO. Avda. Real de Madrid, 16.
COMIDAS C. MORENO. Alta, 66.
COMIDAS PUCHOL. Sanchis Bergón, 24.
LA COVA. Pascual y Genis, 3.
LAS CHECAS. Camino de Carbañal, 1.
ELISEO COLLADO. Conde Montornes, 9.
ESMERALDA. Avda. Gaspar Aguilar, 123.
ESPAÑA. Angel Guimerá, 76.
ESPAÑOL. Pedro Aleixandre, 25.
ESTEVE. Alicante, 3.
GRANJA TURIS. Buen Orden, 15.
LA HABANA. Cádiz, 38.
HOGAR. Avda. Pérez Galdós, 116.
JUAN GARCIA. San José de Calasanz, 19.
JUANEZ. Botellas, 2.
JUCAR. Pelayo, 17.
LEMAN. Camino de Moncada, 38.
LOS MADRILES. Avda. José Antonio, 50.
MAÑEZ. Avda. Ausias March, 21.
LA MARINA. Palayo, 48.
EL MARINO. Juan Verdaguer, 18.
MARTINEZ. Calderón de la Barca, 7.
MAYORAL. Arzobispo Mayoral, 10.
MARCURY. Hernán Cortés, 3.
BODEGAS MESTALLA. Micer Masco, 23.
EL MONCAYO. Matías Perelló, 8.
MONTES. San Francisco de Borja, 19.
NAPOLES. San José de la Montaña, 23.
NINOT. Avda. Pérez Galdós, 147.
OFICINA. Duque de Calabria, 18.
ORTIZ. Mallorquins, 4.
LA PALOMA. Santa Amalia, 6.
EL PARAISO. Avda. Pérez Galdós, 65.
PARIS. Ciscar, 32.
PINARES. Jesús, 80.
LA REJA. Avda. del Puerto, 124.
LA REQUENENSE. San José de Calasanz, 15.
RIA DE VIGO. J.J. Sister, 24.
EL ROMERAL. Ctra. Nacional de Sagunto a Burgos, Km. 4.
LA RONDA. Guillén de Castro, 146.
LA ROSA. Avda. Puerto, 292.
LA SEBA. Pintor Navarro Lloréns, 5.
SENDRA. Avda. Puerto, 178.
SORNI. Ctra. Barcelona, Km. 363.
TABERNA ALCAÑIZ. Bailén, 10.
TABERNA CERVERON. Eugenia Viñes, 115.
TABERNA CON COMIDAS. Santo Cristo del Grao, 16.
TABERNA EL CHOPO. Carcagente, 3.
LOS TRES CASTILLOS. Doctor Romagosa, 19.
TRES HERMANOS. J.J. Domine, 10.
EL TURIA. Bailén, 12.
COMIDAS UTIELANAS. Transits, 8.
VENTA EL TOBOSO. Mar, 22.
LAS VENTAS. Gran Vía de Fernando el Católico, 40.
EL VENTORRO. Bonaire, 8.
LOS VIÑALES. Pintor Fillol, 4.

VIUDA DE MARIANO ANDRES. Avda. General Franco, 23.

Alacuas

LAS PIEDRAS. Paseo de la Ribera, 35.

Albaida

ODON. Ctra. Alcoy, s/n.

Alberique

ROBERTO. Antonio Lloret, 24.

Alboraya

LA PATACONA. Partida de Mar, 48.
BODEGAS POLIT (HIJO). Partida de Vera, 62.
LEVANTE. Partida de Vera, 108.
MERENDERO EL GATO. Partida Masamardá, 43.

Albuixech

PERIS. Avda. Caudillo, 22.

Alcira

MARTINEZ. Reyes Católicos, 77.
CLIMENT. Sangre, 4.
EL MERCAT. Faustino Blasco, 38.
TAKA, SA. Faustino Blasco, 47.

Alcudia de Carlet

LAS CUATRO AROCAS. Ctra. Nacional, Km. 340.
C. EL SERRALLO. Calvo Acacio, s/n.

Alcudia de Crespins

GRAU. Ctra. Madrid, 4.
MANZANO. Ctra. Valencia, 2.

Algemesí

SCOTCH. Montaña, 18.
OCHERA. Plaza del Caudillo, 10.

Alginet

LA BARRACA. Ctra. de Madrid, Km. 25.

Almacera

LOS PEPIN'S. Valencia, 5.

Ayora

SERGIO. Plaza Mártires, 6.

Benetuser

COMIDAS BONESTAR. Avda. Calvo Sotelo, 139.
QUINIELA. Calvo Sotelo, 40.

Benimamet

AMERICANO. Pego, 10.

Beniparrell

CASA QUIQUET. José Antonio, 29.
VALENCIA. José Antonio, 32.

Bocairente

GRACIA. Juan de Juanes, s/n.

Buñol

HAJO-JILTON. Carretera Madrid-Castellón, Km. 313.
ACACIAS. Paseo San Luis, 1.
ZAPATA. Portilla de Buñol, 309.

Burjasot

BENAGEVER. General Aranda, 89.
TRAPERO. Roberto y Villar, 10.
CASA VALERO. Cudillo, 91.

Cauet de Berenguer

MAR BLAU. Playa.

La Cañada

CASA PASCUAL. Plaza del Sol, s/n.
CASA EL ROIG. Plaza del Caudillo, 22.
MONTECAÑADA. Seiscientos dos, s/n.
MERENDERO CALABUIG. Ctra. Cañada, 22.

Carcagente

CASA JESUS. Cte. Hernández, 12.
LA CRUZ. Emilio Donat, 2.

Catarroja

VILLA NUEVA. Ctra. Murcia-Valencia, Km. 240,300.

Candete de las Fuentes

CASA LA ABUELA. Ctra. Madrid-Valencia, 17.
FUENTE CHICA. Ctra. Madrid, 4.

Cuart de Poblet

VENTA DEL AIRE. Ctra. Madrid, Km. 9.

Cullera

CHELO. Valencia, 44.
JOVI. 18 de Julio, 18.
L'ILLA. Punta de la Grúa-Faro Cullera.
MAR DE ORO. Cabañal-Playa, s/n.
MARMOL. Cabañal, 4.
MESON DE CATHARINA. Avda. Cabañal, 40.
LES MOUETTES. Subida al Castillo, s/n.
LA PITERA. Partida del Dosel, s/n.
PURETA. 18 de Julio, 263.
SALVADOR. Partida Estany, s/n.
SAN LORENZO. Ntra. Sra. del Pilar, s/n.
LE TONKIN. Edif. St. Germain.
LA TORRE. Valencia, 1.
ADELA. Maestro Vall, 5.
LA BARRACA. R. don Jaime, 12.
LA BORRASCA. Pl. Fleming Faro, s/n.

CASA TONET. 18 de Julio, 139.
LOS CHICOS. Caminas Dels Homens, 3.
FEDE. Mareny de San Lorenzo, s/n.
MARGA. Peris Mencheta, 1.
LOS OLIVOS. Ctra. del Faro, s/n.
LA PAZ. Alemania, s/n.
PICANTERRA. Estany, s/n.
RONDA. Pl. de España, 18.
TUNEL MARISQUERO. Faro de Cullera, s/n.

Chirivella

MUSTANG. Vicente Lladro Sena, 1.

Chiva

EL CANARIO. Ctra. Madrid-Valencia, Km. 321.
IGNACIO. Ctra. Madrid, Km. 319.
OLIMAR. Ctra. Nacional Madrid-Valencia, Km. 329.

Daimuz

OLIMPICO. Mártires, s/n.
PLAYA DAIMUZ. Playa Daimuz, s/n.

Estivella

ESTIVELLA. Pl. del Generalísimo, 11.

Favareta

RANCHO SAN LUIS. Ctra. Valencia, s/n.
MILLET. Avda. de la Virgen, s/n.
TORRES. De la Virgen, s/n.
SOL. Virgen del Castillo, 1.

Fuente la Higuera

LAS ERAS. Ctra. Comarcal, Km. 320.

Gabarda

VDA. DE ANTONIO GALBIS. Ctra. Real de Madrid, 5.

Gandía

DUCAL. P. de Neptuno, s/n.
CLUB NAUTICO. Paseo Neptuno, 2.
EL MESON DE LOS REYES. Mallorca, 21.
BARRINA. Avda. Neptuno, 1.
BIARRITZ. Atlántico, 7.
CAFE DEL PUERTO. Avda. del Puerto, 19.
CAMPING. Playa de Gandía.
CAMPING ROS. Playa Norte de Gandia, s/n.
ESTRELLA DEL MAR. Mare Nostrum, 3.
MADRIGAL. Mallorca, 18.
MAR LLANTI. Luis Beldá, 18.
MEDITERRANEO. Mallorca, s/n.
RIPOLL. Alcoy, 3.
ROSQUILLA. P. de Neptuno, s/n.
TORO NEGRO. Marqués de Campo, 18.
ALAMEDA. Marqués de Campo, 9.
BUENOS AIRES. Cibeles, 14.
EL CORDOBES. Cánovas del Castillo, 23.
LA ECONOMICA. Ctra. Valencia, 1.
GAMBA. Levante, 7.
MENGUAL. Ctra. Playa.

OLIVERO. Playa-P. de Neptuno.
RANCHO GRANDE. Cibeles, s/n.
VIUDA DE CHIMO. P. de Neptuno, s/n.

El Grao de Gandía

EL BARCO. Del Barco, 15.
TASCA LA NAYA. Ermita, 20.
CASA PACO. Gral. Churruca, 1.
SAN NICOLAS. Río San Nicolás.

Guadasequies

EL FARO. Ctra. Játiva-Ballus.

Jaraco

MONDUBER. Avda. Valencia, s/n.
SOL MAR. Playa de Jaraco, s/n.

Játiva

CASA LA ABUELA. Calle de la Reina 15.
CORREA. Calle de la Reina, 13.

Jeresa

CAMPING CAUDELI. Ctra. Murcia-Valencia Km. 205.

Liria

BORIS. San Vicente, 14.
MONTERO. Plaza del Caudillo, 30.
NAVARRO. Duque de Liria, s/n.
ROMERO. Juan Izquierdo, 67.

Manises

AZAFATA CLUB. Pista Aeropuerto Km. 1.
AEROPUERTO. Aeropuerto Nacional de Manises.

Masalaves

LAS VEGAS. Ctra. Real Madrid, 30.
EL PARAISO. Ctra. Real Madrid, s/n.

Masamagrell

RODRIGO. Generalísimo, 54-56.

Masías

BON AIRE. Calle 123, 4.

Mislata

ALONSO. San Antonio, 150.

Mogente

TORRES. Ctra. Nacional 340, Km. 15.

Montortal

PORTA. Ctra. Real Madrid, s/n.

Naquera

EL PI. Ctra. Burjasot, Km. 18.
MONTEAMOR. Urbanización Monteamor.

Nazaret

VENTA DEL MAR. Punta del Mar, 89.
EL LAGO. Algemesi, 23.

Oliva

CAVALL BERNAT. Ctra. Gandía, s/n.
SIMO. Edificio Rebollet, Ctra. Valencia-Murcia.
APARCADERO CANET. Ctra. Valencia-Almeria, Km. 187.
CAMPING OLE. Partida Aigua Marta, s/n.
CAMPING SAN FERNANDO. Camping San Fernando.
EURO-CAMPING. Partida Randells, s/n.

Onteniente

EL CISNE. Ramón y Cajal, s/n.
REGIO. Dos de Mayo, 1.

El Palmar

ALBUFERA. Juan Bautista Valldecabres, 17.
MATEU. Vicente Baldovi, 19.
PALMAR. General Aranda, 4.
NOSTRE. Juan Bautista Valldecabre, 10.

El Perelló

GUILLERMO. Avda. Narciso Monturiol, s/n.
EL PATO. Mare Nostrum, 3.
FRENTEMAR. Apartamar Frentemar.
PARIS. Bernardo Esteve, 1.
SALAMANCA. Playa del Perelló.

El Perellonet

ALFONSO. Camino Recati, 5.
CASA ALFONSO. Playa de Perellonet, Km. 18.
MARE NOSTRUM. Ctra. Valencia-Oliva.
VERDIBLAU. Ctra. Valencia- Oliva, 72.
VIDAL. Apartamentos Mare Nostrum.
CASA PEDRO. Ctra. Nazaret, 83.

Picasent

SALCAR. Ctra. Alborache-Silla, Km. 28.

Piles

BRISA DEL MAR. Del Mar, 32.

Pinedo

LA ESTRELLA. Playa de Pinedo.
LOS GERANIOS. Playa de Pinedo, s/n.
MEDITERRANEO. Pinedo del Mar, 98.
LA MORENA. Ctra. Montañares, 41.
LAS TRES ROSAS. Travesía Pinedo del Mar, s/n.
TROPICAL. Playa de Pinedo.
EL VELERO. Montañares, 88.

Puebla de Farnals

CARABELAS. Complejo Carabelas.
NOBEL. Complejo Sabas.
MEDITERRANEO. 18 de Julio, 27.

Puebla de Vallbona

LES PROMENADES. Poeta Llorente, 126.

Puig

CASA MARIA. Progreso, 29.
BOLEA. Playa de Puig.

La punta

FABERO. Avda. Mártires, 51.
MARTINOT. Entrada Martinot, 17.

Puzol

ESTRELLA. Ctra. Barcelona, 7.
PUZOL. Barcelona, 41.
EL TURCO. Playa, 6.

Requena

LA ESTRELLA. Plaza General Sanjurjo, 4.
MESON DEL VINO. General Varela, 11.
SAN JOSE. Finca de San José, s/n.
PATILLA. Ctra. Valencia-Madrid, Km. 281.
SOL. Ctra. Nacional III, Km. 281,7.
CORREOS. Nueva Estación, 3.

Ribarroja

TOLEDO. General Varela, 31.

Roca-Meliana

RUFINO. Playa Meliana, s/n.

Sagunto

C. LA PINADA. Ctra. Sagunto-Burgos, Km. 3.
AVENIDA. Avda. José Antonio, 62.
AVENIDA. Generalísimo, 18.
CASA LUIS. Generalísimo, 12.
CUATRO HERMANAS. Ctra. Nacional 340, Km. 19.
MONTECARLO. Aben Barhi, 17.
SOL DEL MAR. Playa de Corinto, s/n.
CAMPING MON-TIBERIO. Playa de Almarda, s/n.
CASA PACO. Avda. Alemania, s/n.
CONTINENTAL. Avda. Generalísimo, s/n.
LOS CHULVIS. La Almarda-Finca Peña, s/n.
NIZA Avda. Generalísimo, 23.
VENTORRILLO DE ROSA. Ctra. Valencia-Barcelona, Km. 30.

El Saler

LA DEHESA. Playa del Saler, 1.
CASA PATILLA. Pinares, 2.
JAIME. Pinares, 6.
PEPE. Pinares, 18.
TABOGA. Pinares, 28.
VICENTE. Pinares, 16.
MERENDERO DE LA ESTRELLA. Playa del Saler.

Siete Aguas

VENTA L'HOME. Ctra. Madrid, Km. 303.

Silla

CASA JULIO. Cuatro Caminos, 10.
MONTECARLO. Puerto, 33.

Sollana

FLORIDA. Generalísimo, 145.

Sueca

BUENOS AIRES. Avda. España, 49 bajo.
CASA CHIVA. Vía Sucronense, 15.
MARENY BLAU. Mareny Blau, s/n.
LAS PALMERAS. Vía San Rost, 2.
SOL, MAR Y NARANJOS. Mareny Barraquetes, s/n.
SUCARSU'S. Ctra. Valencia-Alicante, Km. 232.
EL ABRE. Avda, España, 7.

Tabernes de Valldigna

ALCIMAR. Playa.
BLANCO Y NEGRO. Avda. Playa Tabernes.
BORDERIA. Partida Teularet, 14.
CASA VICTOR. Ctra. Valencia-Alicante, 15.
CINCO HERMANAS. Ctra. Valencia-Alicante, Km. 215.
VENTA CHELO. Ctra. Nacional Valencia-Murcia.

Torrente

EL PORVENIR. Avda. San Lorenzo, 85.
RISKO. Calicanto.
EL ROMERAL. Zona Centro, 37.
EL BARRACON. Zona 1ª, 16.
LA CURRA. Masía del Juez, 77.
EL GRANERO. Masía del Juez, 70.
MERENDERO EL PINO. Avda. San Lorenzo, 86.
LAS PALMERAS. Avda. San Lorenzo, 129.
LA TORRETA. Avda. San Lorenzo, 24.

Utiel

LA ABUELA. Ctra. Madrid-Valencia, Km. 270.
POTEJERO CHICO. Ctra. Madrid-Valencia, Km. 269,500.
ROMERO. Alto San Agustín, s/n.

Venta del Emperador

ROMERO. Ctra. Barcelona, 10.

Villamarchante

MONTE HORQUERA. Urbanización Horquera.

ESPECIALIDADES GASTRONOMICAS

El arroz es la base de la cocina típica valenciana; por su facilidad de combinación da lugar a infinidad de guisos de imposible enumeración aquí. Hacemos sólo referencia al plato que mayor renombre ha alcanzado incluso fuera de las fronteras.

Paella. Plato típico por excelencia; su renombre se debe, sin duda, a que constituye una ponderada y acertada combinación de sanos y nutritivos elementos.

La paella legítima se condimenta en el recipiente metálico que le da nombre, siendo sus ingredientes además del arroz, el pollo, las judías tiernas corrientes y otra variedad originaria de la región llamada «garrofó» (judía alta garrofal) aceite, algo de ajo, pimiento colorado y tomate.

A la orilla del mar, la paella toma pescado y mariscos en lugar de carne no siendo por ello menos suculenta y agradable.

Otra variedad del arroz con pescado, es el arroz abanda o arroz marinera.

All í pebre. En la comarca que circunda el lago La Albufera, se condimentan las anguilas a base de una salsa en cuya composición entran el ajo y la pimienta (all i pebre) y que resulta sabrosísima para los paladares que no desdeñan las sensaciones fuertes.

Dulces. No es posible detallar la lucida gama de dulces con que cuenta la repostería valenciana ya famosa en la antigüedad.

Los tiene distribuidos por variedades vinculadas a las festividades más importantes del año: así por Pascua se confeccionan los «Panquemados»; por Navidad, «Tortas Finas» y «Pastelitos de boniato»; por San Dionisio «Piuletes» y «Tronadors» dulces a base de mazapán; «Tortas Cristinas», «Pasteles de Gloria», «Buñuelos», etc.

ESPECIALITES GASTRONOMIQUES

Le riz est la base de la cuisine typique de Valence; par sa facilité de combinaison, il donne lieu à une à énumérer ici. Nous nous référons à une très grande renommée, même infinité de preparations impossibles à hors des frontières.

Paella. Plat typique par excellence; son renom est dû, sans doute au fait qu'il constitue une combinaison pondérée et appropriée d'éléments sains et nourissants. La paella légitime se condimente dans le récipient métallique qui lui donne son nom, et ses ingrédients, outre le riz sont le poulet, les haricots tendres courants et une autre variété originaire de la région appelée «garrofo» de l'huile, un peu d'ail, du piment rouge et de la tomate.

Au bord de la mer, la paella prend du poisson et des fruits de mer à la place de la viande, sans en perdre sa saveur et son agrément.

Une autre variété du riz au poisson est le riz «abanda» ou marinière.

All i pebre. Dans la région qui entoure le lac La Albufera, on condimente les anguilles avec une sauce dans la composition de laquelle entrent l'ail et le poivre (all i pebre) et qui est très savoureuse pour les palais qui ne dédaignent pas les sensations fortes.

Douceurs. Il n'est pas possible de citer ici toutes les douceurs que comporte la pâtisserie de Valence, déjà fameuse dans l'antiquité.

Elles sont distribuées par variétés liées aux festivités les plus importantes de l'année. Ainsi pour Pâques, on confectionne les «Panquemados», à Noël, «Tortas finas» et «Pastelitos de boniato» pour St. Denis «Piuletes» et «Tronadors» douceurs à base de massepain, «Tortas Cristinas» «Pasteles de Gloria» «Buñuelos», etc.

GASTRONOMIC SPECIALITIES

Rice is the basis of the tropical Valencian dish; as it is so easily combined with many things, it is quite impossible to list the dishes here. We are only going to refer to the best known dish, wich has even reached international fame.

Paella. The par excellence regional dish; its fame is due without doubt to the fact that it consists of a balanced and successfully blended conbination of healthy and nutritive elements.

The legitimate paella is condimented in the metallic container of the same name, the ingredients being, apart from rice chicken, tender green beans, and another variety of the region called «garrofo» (= carob beans), oil, garlic, red peper and tomato.

By the sea the paella is made of fish and shellfish, which does not make the dish any less succulent or pleasant.

Another variety of rice with fish is the «abanda» rice or «marine» rice.

All i pebre. In the region surrounding the Albufera lake, the eels are cooked and served on the basis of a source which consists of garlic and pepper (all i pebre). The result is delicious for those who like strong tasting food.

Sweets. It is not possible to detail the rich range of sweets and cakes typical of Valencia, which were famous in times past.

They are connected with the most important festivities of the pear; at Easter the «Panquemados»; at Christmas «Tortas Finas» and «Pastelitos de boniato»; around San Dionisio «Piuletes» and «Tronadors», «Tortas Cristinas», «Pasteles de Gloria», «Buñuelos», etc.

GASTRONOMISCHE SPEZIALITÄTEN

Der Reis stellt die Grundlage der typisch valencianischen Küche dar. Aufgrund seiner zahlreichen Kombinationsmöglichkeiten wird er in unzähligen Gerichten, die wir hier nicht alle aufzählen können, verwendet. Wir führen hier nur das auch ausserhalb Spaniens berühmteste Gericht auf.

Paella. *Ein vorzügliches und typisches Ge-*
richt, das seinen Ruhm- zweifellos den in
ihm enthaltenen nahrhaften und genau
abgestimmten Bestandteilen verdankt.
Die echte paella *wird in einem Metallgefäss.*
das diesem Gericht seinen Namen gab,
zubereitet. Die Zutaten bestehen ausser
dem Reis aus Hähnchen, zarten grünen
Bohnen und einer anderen Bohnenart die-
ses Gebietes, genannt garrafó, Ol, *etwas*
Knoblauch, roten Paprikaschoten und To-
maten.
In der Nähe des Meeres wird das Fleisch
durch Fisch und Seemuscheln ersetzt, wes-
halb aber die paella *nicht weniguer köstlich*
schmeckt.
Ein weiteres Reisgericht, das Fisch enthält,
ist der sogenannte arroz abanda *oder* arroz
marinera.
All i pebre. *In der Umgebung der* Albufera
würzt man die Aale mit einer Sosse aus
Knoblauch und Pfeffer (all i pebre), die
besonders die vorziehen, deren Gaumen und
Magen Pikantes vertragen.
Süsspeisen. *Wir können hier leider nicht*
alle Spezialitäten der valencianischen Kon-
ditoreien, die schon im Altertum einen
Namen hatten, aufzählen.
Zu jedem Fest gibt es die entsprechenden
Süssigkeiten; so zum Beispiel zu Ostern
die «Panquemados», *Weihnachten* «Tortas
Finas» *(Torten) und* «Pastelitos de boniato»,
zum Nanensfest des heiligen Dionys «Piule-
tes» *und* «Tronadors» *(Süssigkeiten aus*
Marzipan); ferner «Tortas Cristinas» *«Paste-*
les de Gloria», «Buñuelos» *usw.*

CAFETERIAS—CAFETERIAS
CAFES—KAFFEE

ANFRA. Avellanas, 9. Telf. 22 98 07.
ARIES. Cuarte, 119. Telf. 26 71 99.
ASINS. Cobertizo San Pablo, 1. Telf. 22 97 90.
BAHIA. Jesús, 8. Telf. 22 44 42.
BALDO. Ribera, 5. Telf. 22 98 61.
BARBI. Serranos, 21. Telf. 31 10 03.
BARCELONA. Avda. Ramiro Ledesma, 39. Telf.65 50 57.
BARRANOVA. Játiva, 30. Telf. 22 22 21.
BINPY. G. V. Marq. Turia, 3. Telf. 22 64 04.
BRASILIA. Paz, 31. Telf. 22 95 77.
VALIENTE. Plaza Ruzafa, 8. Telf. 27 38 32.
CARRUSEL. P. Portada, 16. Telf. 23 22 35.
CARTAGO. Avda. P. y Valero, 175. Telf. 33 50 74.
CATANIA. Avda. José Antonio, 16. Telf, 33 10 67.
YUCA. Mar, 42. Telf. 22 99 84.
COLOMBIA. Gral. Prim, 17. Telf. 33 50 73.
COSTA MARFIL. Gran Vía Marqués Turia, 29. Telf. 22 98 63
COVALTA. G. V. Marqués Turia, 44. Telf. 33 11 79.
CHILE. Beata, 6. Telf. 22 96 05.
DAKAR. G. Castro, 89. Telf. 31 50 91.

DEL MARINO. Pl. Div. Azul, 3. Telf. 23 22 12.
DUERO. Játiva, 12. Telf. 22 96 44.
EL TOSTADERO. Avda. B. Cárcer, 31. Telf. 22 99 00.
EL ZORRO. Avda. J. Benavente, 1. Telf. 33 10 37.
FRANCIA. Calixto III, 35. Telf. 25 50 33.
GALERIAS. Avda. Barón Cárcer, 48. Telf. 22 98 86.
GRAU. Ramón y Cajal, 4. Telf. 22 96 25.
GRECIA. G. V. F. Católico, 30. Telf. 31 50 93.
GUADARRAMA. G. V. Fernando Católico, 2. Telf. 22 98 16.
HUNGARIA. C. Sotelo, 3. Telf. 22 97 37.
INCA. Calvo Sotelo, 22. Telf. 21 46 73.
JAMAICA. Avda. J. Benavente, 8. Telf. 33 11 94.
JERO. Conv. Sta. Clara, 3. Telf. 22 96 41.
JEYDI. Avda. Cid, 54. Telf. 25 50 66.
JIMELIA. L. de Rueda, 2. Telf. 31 50 28.
JUNCO. Ruzafa, 27. Telf. 22 97 71.
KANSAS. Campaneros, 20. Telf. 22 98 04.
LA CABAÑA. J. Verdaguer, 10. Telf. 23 36 77.
LA LLAVE. Gran Vía Marqués Turia, 59. Telf. 22 99 70.
LA PAZ. Paz, 37. Telf. 22 96 61.
LA VERJA. Bailén, 18. Telf. 22 98 38.
LAS DAMAS. Damas, 3. Telf. 22 99 21.
LAS PALMERAS. Albacete, 1. Telf. 25 50 82.
LAS TORRES. G. de Castro, 121. Telf. 31 40 28.
LAURIA. Roger de Lauria, 2. Telf. 22 98 06.
LEBUK. Avda. P. Reig, 145. Telf. 69 30 08.
LIBANO. Colón, 42. Telf. 22 99 47.
LONDRES. Avda. del Cid, 90. Telf. 26 10 97.
LORCA. Lorca, 5. Telf. 26 10 34.
MASCARELL. Lérida, 10. Telf. 65 30 49.
MONTERREY. Abadía S. Martín, 2. Telf. 22 89 59.
MONTEVERDE. Avda. José Antonio, 88. Telf. 33 10 83.
NADAL. Vicente Brull, 17. Telf. 23 23 38.
NEVADA. G. V. Fernando el Católico, 53. Telf. 25 51 21.
NILO. Avda. José Antonio, 59. Telf. 34 11 45.
OESTE. Avda. B. de Cárcer, 44. Telf. 22 96 93.
OSLO. S. Sivera, 8. Telf. 26 11 74.
PALMA. M. Bellver, 1. Telf. 25 50 63.
PAQUI-MAR. Astilleros, 77. Telf. 23 23 92.
PARIS. Mediterráneo, 23. Telf. 23 23 55.
PEGUSOVA. E. José Capuz, 15. Telf. 33 51 41.
PLAZA. Pl. P. Segrelles, 7. Telf. 26 10 79.
POKER. Avda. Primado Reig, 40. Telf. 65 50 99.
RENO. Roger Lauria, 10. Telf. 22 97 69.
REUS. Reus, 2. Telf. 65 50 26.
REX. G. V. Mqs. de Sotelo, 1. Telf. 21 13 66.
RIPALDA. Sogueros, 7. Telf. 31 10 38.
RIVIERA. Pintor Sorolla, 22. Telf. 22 96 15.
ROMA. Plaza Virgen, 4. Telf. 31 10 60.
ROYAL. G. V. R. y Cajal, 3. Telf. 26 10 67.
SALVINATA. Pilar, 1. Telf. 22 99 02.
SAN CARLOS. Castán Tobeñas, 1. Telf. 25 72 88.
SAN CRISTOBAL. Plaza América, 4. Telf. 22 77 91.

SAN FRANCISCO. Comedias, 24. Telf. 22 97 00.
SAN REMO. S. A. Játiva, 23. Telf. 22 98 10.
SANTANA. Comedias, 1. Telf. 22 58 59.
SUESBA. San Vicente, 12. Telf. 21 19 08.
SUIZO. H. Chabás, 3. Telf. 22 96 62.
TOKIO. C. Amorós, 51. Telf. 22 97 56.
VALIENTE. Avda. Pérez Galdós, 91. Telf. 25 51 72.
VICTORIA. Ruzafa, 42. Telf. 33 50 62.
3. H. Mallorquins, 1. Telf. 22 74 19.
COLON. Colón, 18. Telf. 22 99 73.

LIBRERIAS—LIBRAIRIES
BOOKSHOPS—BUCHHANDLUNGEN

LIBRERIA ALEGRE. Juan Llorens, 60.
LIBRERIA AUROMAR. Dr. Sumsi, 2.
LIBRERIA BELLO. Barcas, 5.
LIBRERIA EUGENIO. Blasco Calatrava, 4.
LIBRERIA CIENTIFICO. Médica Sanz, 5.
PAPELERIA CLIMENT. Vila Jesús, 4.
LIBRERIA CHIRIVILLA. Guillén de Castro, 25.
LIBRERIA DANIEL. José Benlliure,267.
LIBRERIA DAVILA. Sangre, 9.
LIBRERIA DELIBER. Cardenal Benlloch.
PAPELERIA DURA. Maestro Clave, 2.
LIBRERIA ROBERTO. Elías San Vicente, 77.
LIBRERIA GALINDO. José Benlliure, 118.
LIBRERIA RAFAEL. Gallur Pelayo, 51.
LIBRERIA GARCIA. Muñoz Lorca, 7.
LIBRERIA GEMUS. Pintor Sorolla, 15.
LIBRERIA IDEAS. Marqués de Turia, 21.
LIBRERIA LAURIA. Lauria, 7.
LIBRERIA MANANTIAL. Paz, 7.
LIBRERIA MARAGUAT. Pl. del Caudillo, 22.
LIBRERIA A. MOLINER. Fernando el Católico, 57.
LIBRERIA JESUS ORTEGA. S. Vicente, 76.
LIBRERIA PARIS VALENCIA. Pelayo, 7.
LIBRERIA VICENTE PONT PORTELA. Convento Santa Clara, 9.
LIBRERIA BENIGNO PORTELO. Convento San Francisco, 4.
LIBRERIA REAL. Correjeria, 20.
LIBRERIA SAN PABLO. Campaneros, 16.
LIBRERIA MANUEL SOTO MARTI. Carricola, 10.
LIBRERIA TECNICA. Luis Santangel, 1.
LIBRERIA TECNICA EXTRANJERA. Paz, 35.
LIBRERIA TELIO. Marqués de Turia, 9.
LIBRERIA HERMINIO VANACLOCHA. Milagro, 4.

CORREOS, TELEGRAFOS Y
TELEFONOS

CORREOS. Administración Principal. Plaza del Caudillo, 24. Telf. 21 12 35.
TELEGRAFOS. Oficina Central, en el mismo de Correos. Telf. 21 73 40.
TELEFONOS. Plaza del Caudillo, 25. Telf. 004.

POSTES, TELEGRAPHES
ET TELEPHONES

POSTES. Administration Principale. Plaza del Caudillo, 24. Telf. 21 12 35.
TELEGRAPHES. Bureau central, le même que la poste. Telf. 21 73 40.
TELEPHONES. Plaza del Caudillo, 25. Telf. 004 et 21 73 40.

POST OFFICE, TELEGRAPHS
AND TELEPHONES

POST OFFICE. Headquarters: Plaza del Caudillo, 24. Telf. 21 12 35.
TELEGRAPH OFFICE. Head Office, in the Post Office. Telf. 21 73 40.
TELEPHONES. Plaza del Caudillo, 25. Telf. 004

POST-, TELEGRAPHEN- UND
FERNSPRECHAMT

POSTAMT. Hauptverwaltung. Plaza del Caudillo 24. Telf. 21 12 35.
TELEGRAPHENAMT. Zentralbüro im Gebäude der Hauptpost. Telf. 21 73 40.
FERNSPRECHAMT. Plaza del Caudillo 25. Telf. 004.

CENTROS OFICIALES
CENTRES OFFICIELS
OFFICIAL CENTRES
BEHÖRDEN

AYUNTAMIENTO. Plaza del Caudillo, 1. Telf. 22 01 90.
DIPUTACION PROVINCIAL. Caballeros, 2. Telf. 31 37 90.
GOBIERNO CIVIL. Plaza del Temple, 1. Telf. 21 12 80.
GOBIERNO MILITAR. Calle de Justicia, 8. Telf. 22 52 81.
CAPITANIA GENERAL. Plaza de Tetuán, 22. Telf. 22 06 95.
DELEGACION PROVINCIAL DEL MINISTERIO DE INFORMACION Y TURISMO. Paz, 17. Telf. 22 86 93.
OFICINA DE INFORMACION DE LA SUBSECRETARIA DE TURISMO. Paz, 46. Telf. 21 25 85.
OFICINA DE INFORMACION DE LA SUBSECRETARIA DE TURISMO. Aeropuerto de Manises.
SOCIEDAD VALENCIANA FOMENTO DEL TURISMO. Bajos del Ayuntamiento. Telf. 21 76 90.
OFICINA MUNICIPAL DE TURISMO. La misma dirección anterior.
JEFATURA SUPERIOR DE POLICIA. Gran Vía de Ramón y Cajal, 40. Telf. 21 45 73.
COCHES PATRULLA. Telf. 21 31 81.
JEFATURA PROVINCIAL DE TRAFICO. Plaza del Temple, 1. Telf. 21 12 11.

REAL AUTOMOVIL CLUB DE VALENCIA. Avenida de Jacinto Benavente, 25. Telf. 27 01 60.
TURING CLUB DE ESPAÑA. Avenida del Barón de Cárcer, 48. Telf. 21 01 72.
CASAS DE SOCORRO. Colón: Avenida Navarro Reverter, 11. Telf. 21 25 44, 22 18 68. Levante: Doctor Lluch, 4 (El Grao). Telf. 23 03 04. Museo: Puente de San José. Telf. 31 16 47. Ruzafa: Matías Perelló, 7. Telf. 27 45 15.

AGENCIAS DE VIAJES
AGENCES DE VOYAGE
TRAVEL AGENCIES
REISEGESELLSCHAFTEN

VIAJES ORTEGA. Gran Vía Ramón y Cajal, 6. Telf. 21 77 62.
VIAJES BRIO. Paz, 1. Telf. 22 75 38.
VIAJES ESPLAY. Plaza de Alfonso el Magnánimo, 10. Telf. 22 66 74.
VIAJES PERSIVAL. Navellos, 9. Telf. 31 28 34.
VIAJES SICANIA. Ribera, 1. Telf. 22 63 14.
VIAJES BAKUMAR. Cirilo Amorós, 57. Telf. 22 42 22.
VIAJES CONDE. Paz, 37. Telf. 21 79 14.
VIAJES HISPANIA. Pintor Sorolla, 16. Telf. 22 42 80.
VIAJES INTERNACIONAL EXPRESO. Játiva, 21. Telf. 22 17 00.
VIAJES MARSANS. Plaza del Caudillo, 15. Telf. 22 06 99.
VIAJES MARTHE. Paz, 32. Telf. 21 77 35.
VIAJES MELIA. Paz, 41. Telf. 22 33 90.
VIAJES TABER, S. A. Convento de Jerusalén, 1. Telf. 22 98 87.
VIAJES UNIVERSAL. Calvo Sotelo, 20. Telf. 21 03 35.
VIAJES VIKING. Conde de Altea, 26. Telf. 33 43 34.
VIAJES WAGONS-LITS & COOK. Marqués de Sotelo, 7. Telf. 21 16 44.
VIAJES WASTEELS. Julio Antonio, 28. Telf. 22 66 02.
VIAJES VIBLIA. Garriques, 3. Telf. 22 89 89.
VIAJES VALENCIA TRAVEL. Sangre, 9. Telf. 22 73 76.
VIAJES ESPAÑA MUNDIAL. Gran Vía y Ramón y Cajal, 27. Telf. 25 27 58.

COMUNICACIONES
COMMUNICATIONS
COMMUNICATIONS
VERKEHRSVERBINDUNGEN

Estaciones de Ferrocarril
Stations de Chemin de Fer
Railway Stations
Bahnhöfe

ESTACION DEL NORTE. Calle de Játiva. Líneas: Valencia-Cuenca-Madrid; Valencia-Alcázar-Madrid; Valencia-Castellón-Tarragona-Barcelona; Valencia-Alicante-Murcia-Cartagena-Granada; Valencia-Zaragoza (Taf.)
ESTACION DE ARAGON. Plaza de Aragón. Línea: Valencia-Teruel-Zaragoza.
ESTACION FERROCARRILES ELECTRICOS. Orilla del Río. Líneas: Valencia-Grao; Valencia-Liria; Valencia-Rafelbuñol; Valencia-Bétera.
ESTACION VILLANUEVA DE CASTELLON. Calle de Jesús. Línea: Valencia- Villanueva de Castellón.

Líneas aéreas—Lignes aeriennes
Air lines—Luftfahrtgesellschaften

Servicios directos o combinados con Madrid, Barcelona, Palma de Mallorca, Sevilla, Santiago, Canarias, Argel, Orán, París, Bruselas, Londres (directo), etc. Informes:
COMPAÑIA AEREA DE TRANSPORTES IBERIA. Paz, 14. Telf. 21 44 95.
BRITISH EUROPEAN AIRWAYS (B. E. A.) Hermanas Chabás, 8. Telf. 22 97 36.
AVIACION Y COMERCIO, S. A. Paz, 14. Telf. 21 44 95.

Líneas marítimas
Lignes maritimes
Maritime lines
Schiffahrtsgesellschaften

Existen líneas regulares de Valencia a Palma de Mallorca, Ibiza y Canarias, además de otros servicios de cabotaje que la unen con casi todos los puertos de la península. Para detalles:
AUCONA. Paz, 31. Telf. 21 72 47.
COMPAÑIA TRASATLANTICA. Mar, 55. Telf. 21 39 20.
YBARRA Y CIA. C. C. Avenida del Doncel Luis Felipe García-Sanchiz, 338. Telf. 23 09 61.
NAVIERA PINILLOS. Plaza de Alfonso el Magnánimo, 13. Telf. 22 21 49.

Autobuses—Autobus
Buses—Buslinien

Líneas regulares a:
MADRID. Albireque, 15. Telf. 25 41 27.
SEVILLA. Gran Vía Fernando el Católico, 38. Telf. 22 97 09.
ALMERIA. Játiva, 4. Telf. 21 86 68.
ALICANTE. Játiva, 4. Telf. 21 86 68.
CASTELLON. Gran Vía Ramón y Cajal, 3. Telf. 25 53 90.
CUENCA. Calle de Vives Liern, 9. Telf. 21 23 70.
MURCIA. Gran Vía de Germanías, 10. Telf. 27 69 04.
PARIS. Bailén, 2. Telf. 22 26 95.

TAXIS

CENTRAL LLAMADAS. Telf. 69 18 00

DESPACHO DE BILLETES
VENTE DE BILLETS
TICKET OFFICE
FAHRKARTENSCHALTER

AVIACION. Iberia y Aviaco. Paz, 14. Telf. 21 44 95.
MARITIMAS. Aucona. Paz, 29. Telf. 21 72 47 y Estación Marítima (Puerto). Telf. 23 36 88.
FERROCARRIL. Renfe (Oficina de Viajes y Despacho de Billetes). Plaza de Alfonso el Magnánimo, 2. Telf. 21 30 04. Y en las agencias de viajes.

TALLERES DE REPARACION
DE AUTOMOVILES
Agencias oficiales
ATELIERS DE REPARATION
D'AUTOMOBILES
Agences officielles
CAR REPAIR GARAGES
Official agencies
AUTOREPARATURWERKSTÄTTEN
Offizialle Agenturen

CITROEN. Ferrocarril, s/n. Junto cochera tranvía del Camino de El Grao. Telf. 69 39 00.
FORD. Almirante Cadarso, 3. Telf. 27 87 07.
DODGE SIMCA. SEIDA. Ciscar, 37.
D. K. W. Sorní, 29. Telf. 21 85 53.
DODGE SIMCA. Juan Giner Ballester. Avenida Peris y Valera, 141, 143.
CHRYSLER, DE SOTO, HILLMAN, HUMBER, M. G., SUNBEAM, VOLSWAGEN. Ciscar, 33. Telf. 27 41 04.
PEUGEOT VOLVO. Ciscar, 18. Telf. 27 06 11.
MERCEDES BENZ, PANHARD. Camino de Barcelona, 119. Telf. 21 86 39.
AUSTIN. Doctor Sumsi, 38. Telf. 27 47 15.
BORGWARD. Sueca, 67. Telf. 27 65 24.
FIAT, SEAT. San Vicente, 85-87. Telf. 21 44 35.
LAND ROVER, BEDFORD, BUICK, CADILLAC, CHEVROLET, OLDSMOBILE, OPEL, PONTIAC, VAUXHALL. Almirante Cadarso, 15. Telf. 27 84 37.
LAMBRETA, MOBYLETTE. Conde de Salvatierra, 43. Telf. 21 30 39.
VESPA. (Ver Fiat).
NEUMATICOS MICHELIN. Avda. de Pérez Galdós, 82. Telf. 25 88 05.
NEUMATICOS FIRESTONE. Avda. del Cardenal Benlloch, 71. Telf. 69 25 50.
NEUMATICOS PIRELLI. Ctra. de Torrente, s/n. Telf. 79 14 50.
NEUMATICOS GENERAL. Almirante Cadarso, 8. Telf. 27 04 46.

ESTACIONES DE SERVICIO
STATIONS SERVICE
PETROL STATIONS
TANKSTELLEN MIT SERVICE

VALENCIA. Avda. Ramiro Ledesma, 273.
VALENCIA. Camino Real de Madrid, Km. 1.
VALENCIA. Avda. del Cid, 3.
VALENCIA. Avda. de Campanar, 41.
VALENCIA. Avda. del Doncel Luis Felipe, García Sanchiz.
VALENCIA. Ctra. Nazaret a Oliva, Km. 7,9.
VALENCIA. Avda. de Doncel Luis Felipe García Sanchiz, 1.
VALENCIA. Ctra. Valencia-Barcelona, Km. 3,1.
VALENCIA. Avda. Jaime Roig.
VALENCIA. Gran Vía Marqués de Turia.
VALENCIA. Calle Cádiz, 100.
VALENCIA. Avda. José Antonio, 83.
VALENCIA. Ctra. Valencia-Paterna, Km. 1,6.
VALENCIA. Avda. Ausias March, s/n.
VALENCIA. Llano de la Zaisia, 4.
VALENCIA. Calle Vives Liern, 3.
ALBAIDA. Ctra. Murcia-Valencia, Km. 161.
ALBERIQUE. Ctra. Murcia-Valencia, Km.206,2.
ALCIRA. Ctra. Alcira-Favareta, Km. 0,4.
ALCUDIA DE CARLET. Ctra. Madrid-Valencia, Km. 216.
ALCUDIA DE CRESPINS. Ctra. Valencia-Madrid, Km. 43,6.
ALGEMESI. Ctra. Sueca-Alberique, Km. 12,3.
ALGEMESI. Ctra. Alcira-Silla. Km. 5,1.
ALGEMESI. Ctra. Játiva-Silla, Km. 25,5
AYORA. Ctra. Almansa-Requena, Km. 23,4.
BENETUSER. Ctra. Valencia-Casas Campillo.
BENIFAYO. Ctra. Murcia-Valencia, Km. 227,7.
BETERA. Ctra. Buriasot-Torres Torres, Km. 10,4.
BONREPOS. Ctra. Valencia-Barcelona, Km. 4,9.
BUÑOL. Ctra. Madrid-Valencia, Km. 313,6.
BURJASOT. Ctra. Valencia-Ademuz, Km. 4,5.
BURJASOT. Calle Valencia, 4.
CARCAGENTE. Calle Sta. Bárbara, 1-15.
CASINOS. Ctra. Valencia-Ademuz, Km. 38,2.
CATADAU. Ctra. Tabernes-Liria, Km. 40,1.
CATARROJA. Ctra. Murcia-Valencia, Km. 240,3.
CUART DE POBLET. Ctra. Madrid-Valencia, Km. 340,8.
CUART DE POBLET. Ctra. Madrid-Valencia, Km. 343,7.
CULLERA. Ctra. Murcia-Valencia, Km. 227,8.
CHESTE, Ctra. Cheste a la N. 111, Km. 1,4.
CHIRIVELLA. Ctra. Mistislata-Peal, Km. 3,4.
CHIVA. Ctra. Madrid-Valencia, Km. 320,6.
ENGUERA. Ctra. Ayora-Gandía, Km. 49,3.
FUENTE LA HIGUERA. Ctra. Casas de Campillo-Valencia, Km. 12,1.
GANDIA. Ctra. Valencia, esq. Colón.
GANDIA. Calle San Rafael, 5.
GANDIA. Calle Canalejas, 55.
GUADASEQUIES. Ctra. Murcia-Valencia, Km. 174,5.
JATIVA. Avda. Selgas, s/n.

JATIVA. Avda. Selgas, 1.
LIRIA. Ctra. Valencia-Ademuz, Km. 27,1.
MANISES. Ctra. Madrid-Valencia-Villamar-chante.
MANISES. Ctra. Cuart de Poblet-Domeño, Km. 2,3.
MASANASA. Ctra. Murcia-Valencia, Km. 242,1.
MISLATA. Ctra. Madrid-Valencia, Km. 348.
MOGENTE. Ctra. Casas Campillo-Valencia, Km. 25,9.
MONCADA. Avda. del Seminario.
MONTSERRAT. Ctra. Torrente-Montroig, Km. 21,8.
MUSEROS. Ctra. Valencia-Barcelona, Km. 12,12.
OLIVA. Ctra. Murcia-Valencia, Km. 193,8.
ONTENIENTE. Ctra. Villena-Alcudia, Km. 38,7.
ONTENIENTE. Ctra. Almansa-Grao de Gandía, Km. 50,6.
PATERNA. Ctra. Valencia- Adamuz, Km. 10,1.
PATERNA. Ctra. Paterna-Adamuz, Km. 4,9.
PATERNA. Ctra. Valencia-Adamuz, Km. 13,9.
PEDRALVA. Ctra. Cuarte-Domeño, Km. 30,7.
EL PERELLO. Ctra. Nazaret-Oliva, Km. 20,1.
PICASENT. Ctra. Alborache-Silla, Km. 29,9.
PINEDO. Ctra. Valencia-Saler, Km. 6.
PUZOL. Ctra. Valencia-Barcelona, Km. 18,2.
REQUENA. Ctra. Madrid-Castellón, Km. 281,6.
RIBARROJA DEL TURIA. Ctra. Cuart-Poblet a Domeño, Km. 13,1.
SAGUNTO. Ctra. Sagunto-Puerto Sagunto, Km. 4,2.
SAGUNTO. Ctra. Sagunto-Teruel, Km. 3,1.
SILLA. Ctra. Madrid-Valencia, Km. 236,6.
SILLA. Ctra. Almería-Valencia, Km. 254,1.
SUECA. Ctra. Murcia-Valencia, Km. 233,3.
SUECA. Ctra. Murcia-Valencia, Km. 234.
SUECA. Ctra. Sueca-Perelló, Km. 0,4.
SUECA. Ctra. Murcia-Valencia, Km. 233,3.
TABERNES DE VALLDIGNA. Ctra. Murcia-Valencia, Km. 215,2.
TORRENTE. Avda. San Luis y Calle 18 de Julio.
UTIEL. Ctra. Madrid-Valencia, Km. 268,1.
UTIEL. Ctra. Madrid-Valencia, Km. 270,8.
VENTA QUEMADA. Ctra. Madrid-Valencia, Km.301,5.
VILLAR DEL ARZOBISPO. Ctra. Valencia-Villar, Km. 4.
VILLAGORDO DEL CABRIEL. Ctra. Madrid-Valencia, Km. 263.

TEATROS Y CINES
THEATRES ET CINES
THEATERS AND CINEMAS
THEATER UND KINOS

PRINCIPAL. Barcas, 15. Telf. 21 40 18.
ALCAZAR. General San Martín, 17. Telf. 21 54 43.
APOLO. Don Juan de Austria, 8. Telf. 21 47 04.
RUZAFA. Calvo Sotelo, 23. Telf. 21 40 06.
CAPITOL. Ribera, 16. Telf. 21 55 29.

LYS. Calvo Sotelo, 3. Telf. 21 59 99.
OLYMPIA. San Vicente, 52, Telf. 21 73 15.
REX. Marqués de Sotelo, 6. Telf. 22 06 73.
RIALTO. Plaza del Caudillo, 17. Telf. 25 85 21.
ESLAVA. Calvo Sotelo, 11. Telf. 22 65 65.
LAURIA. Colón, 27. Telf. 22 96 10.
OESTE. Hospital, 1. Telf. 22 88 62.
SERRANO. Calvo Sotelo, 30. Telf. 21 79 57.
ARTIS. Calvo Sotelo, 30. Telf. 21 79 57.
MARTI. Avenida José Antonio, 29. Telf. 27 21 60.

SALAS DE FIESTAS—CABARETS
NIGHT CLUBS—TANZLOKALE

LA BRUJA. Hotel Astoria.
VIVEROS. Restaurante Viveros.
RINCON ESPAÑOL. Salvá, 1. Telf. 22 99 67.
COLMAO. Doctor Manuel Candela, 6. Telf. 23 36 90.

PLAZAS DE TOROS
ARENES—BULLRINGS
STIERKAMPFARENAS

PLAZA DE TOROS. Játiva, 28. Telf. 21 93 15.
VENTA DE «EL SALER». Playa de El Saler.

CLUBS Y SOCIEDADES
DEPORTIVAS
CLUBS ET SOCIETES SPORTIVES
CLUBS AND SPORTS SOCIETIES
CLUBS UND SPORTCLUBS

Campos de fútbol de Mestalla, del Valencia C. F. Avenida de Suecia, s/n. Telf. 33 53 30.
Campo de fútbol de Vallejo de U. D. Levante. Poeta Bodría, 6. Telf. 35 08 00.
CLUB NAUTICO. Restaurante, piscina, embarcadero. Paseo de Caro (Puerto), s/n. Telf. 23 39 84, 23 03 63 y 23 23 15.
LAS ARENAS. Baños de mar, piscina, restaurante. Playa de Levante. Telf. 23 07 53 y 23 07 91.
PISCINA VALENCIA. Federación Valenciana de Natación. Arquitecto Mora, s/n. Telf. 33 26 90.
CLUB PESCADORES DEPORTIVOS. Salvador, 5. Telf. 21 46 10.
CLUB DE TENIS VALENCIA. Botánico Cavanilles, s/n. Telf. 35 38 12.
CLUB ESPAÑOL DE TENIS. Camino Hondo del Grao, 26. Telf. 69 20 03.
REAL SOCIEDAD DE TIRO DE PICHON. Paz, 4. Telf. 21 18 94. Chalet y campo de tiro en playa de Levante. Telf. 23 01 71.
REAL AUTOMOVIL CLUB DE VALENCIA. Avda. de Jacinto Benavente, 25. Telf. 33 30 85, 27 01 60 y 27 99 24.
AERO CLUB DE VALENCIA. Luis Vives, 6. Telf. 21 59 91.
TRINQUETE DE PELAYO. (Juego de pelota valenciana). Pelayo, 8. Telf. 21 26 78.

CLUB DE GOLF (Manises). Telf. 25 63 90. (Centralilla de Aviación). Oficinas en Valencia: Vives Liern, 6. Telf. 21 59 91.
CENTRO EXCURSIONISTA. Caballeros, 21. Telf. 22 16 43.
SOCIEDAD PROVINCIAL DE CAZADORES DE VALENCIA. Telf. 21 24 23.

CONSULADOS
CONSULATS
CONSULATES
KONSULATE

ALEMANIA. Avenida Oeste, 23. Telf. 21 84 05.
ARGENTINA. Colón, 48. Telf. 21 80 98.
BELGICA. Gran Vía Marqués del Turia, 73. Telf. 22 76 74.
BOLIVIA. Lauria, 10. Telf. 31 14 06.
BRASIL. María Cristina, 11. Telf. 22 28 90.
COLOMBIA. Hernán Cortés, 18. Telf. 21 32 68.
COSTA RICA. Gran Vía Germanías, 51. Telf. 23 57 38.
CHILE. Embajador Vich, 11. Telf. 22 14 29.
DINAMARCA. Cirilo Amorós, 70. Telf. 21 36 06.
REPUBLICA DOMINICANA. Mestre Racional, 6. Telf. 27 75 55.
ECUADOR. Pl. Alfonso el Magnánimo, 1. Telf. 22 55 05.
ESTADOS UNIDOS DE AMERICA. Colón, 74. Telf. 21 11 08.
EL SALVADOR. Conde de Salvatierra, 6. Telf. 21 58 77.
FINLANDIA. Plaza de Tetuán, 23. Telf. 21 58 77.
FRANCIA. Cirilo Amorós, 50. Telf. 21 44 94.
GRAN BRETAÑA. Cronista Carreres, 1. Telf. 21 12 75.
GRECIA. Gran Vía Marqués del Turia, 78. Telf. 27 12 39.
GUATEMALA. Ribera, 14. Telf. 21 08 45.
HAITI. Lauria, 30. Telf. 21 57 81.
HONDURAS. Avda. María Cristina, 9. Telf. 21 38 18.
ISLANDIA. Plaza Marqués de Estella, 4. Telf. 21 56 25.
ITALIA. Cirilo Amorós, 46. Telf. 21 15 12.
LIBERIA. Avda. Jacinto Benavente, 18. Telf. 27 67 71.
MONACO. María Cristina, 1. Telf. 21 47 95.
NICARAGUA. Marqués de Sotelo, 1. Telf. 22 47 17.
NORUEGA. Avda. Puerto, 336. Telf. 23 08 97.
PAISES BAJOS. Avenida del Puerto, 269. Telf. 23 00 07.
PERU. Horno de San Nicolás, 8. Telf. 21 99 13.
PORTUGAL. Salvador, 24. Telf. 21 10 24.
SUECIA. Pintor Sorolla, 4. Telf. 22 24 89.
SUIZA. Moratín, 11. Telf. 21 59 33.
URUGUAY. Avda. de José Antonio, 2. Telf. 27 24 36.
VENEZUELA. Avda. de José Antonio, 8. Telf. 27 45 79.

BANCOS—BANQUES
BANKS—BANKEN

BANCO DE ARAGON. Martínez Cubells, 3 y 5. Telf. 21 31 62.
BANCO DE BILBAO. Pintor Sorolla, 15. Telf. 22 29 90.
BANCO CENTRAL. Barcas, 6. Telf. 21 31 30.
BANCO COCA. Martínez Cubells, 11. Telf. 22 89 90.
BANCO COMERCIAL TRASATLANTICO. Lauria, 5. Telf. 22 47 93.
BANCO DE ESPAÑA. Correos, 11. Telf. 21 44 45.
BANCO ESPAÑOL DE CREDITO. Pintor Sorolla, 17. Telf. 21 13 70.
BANCO DE LA EXPORTACION. Pascual y Genís, 2. Telf. 22 08 35.
BANCO EXTERIOR DE ESPAÑA. Pintor Sorolla, 1. Telf. 21 31 96.
BANCO GENERAL DEL COMERCIO Y LA INDUSTRIA. Colón, 2. Telf. 21 85 64.
BANCO HIPOTECARIO DE ESPAÑA. Salvá, 1. Telf. 21 30 77.
BANCO HISPANO AMERICANO. Barcas, 8. Telf. 22 54 80.
BANCO DE LONDRES Y AMERICA DEL SUR.
BANK OF LONDON Y SOUTH AMERICA. Pascual y Genís, 22. Telf. 21 31 00.
BANCO MERCANTIL E INDUSTRIAL. San Vicente, 24. Telf. 22 79 67.
BANCO DE NUESTRA SEÑORA DE LOS DESAMPARADOS. Trinitarios, 3. Telf. 22 34 31.
BANCO POPULAR ESPAÑOL. Barcas, 3. Telf. 22 09 90.
BANCO RURAL Y MEDITERRANEO. Correos, 8. Telf. 22 67 95.
BANCO DE SANTANDER. Calvo Sotelo, 3. Telf. 21 25 25.
BANCO DE VALENCIA. Pintor Sorolla, 2. Telf. 22 03 90.
BANCO VITALICIO DE ESPAÑA. Plaza del Caudillo, 29. Telf. 22 76 46.
BANCO DE VIZCAYA. Plaza del Caudillo, 9. Telf. 22 30 90.
BANCO ZARAGOZANO. Plaza del Caudillo, 28. Telf. 22 00 65.
CAJA DE AHORROS Y MONTE DE PIEDAD. General Tovar, 3. Telf. 21 13 52.
SOCIETE GENERALE DE BANQUE. Plaza del Caudillo, 27. Telf. 21 45 68.

CENTROS DE ENSEÑANZA
CENTRES D'ENSEIGNEMENT
TEACHING CENTRES
LEHRANSTALTEN

UNIVERSIDAD. (Rectorado, oficinas generales y Biblioteca general). Nave, 7. Telf. 21 73 80 (centralita).
FACULTAD DE FILOSOFIA Y LETRAS. Nave, 7. Telf. 22 50 60. (El nuevo edificio, en construcción en el Paseo al Mar).

FACULTAD DE CIENCIAS. Paseo al Mar, 13. Telf. 69 04 62, 69 04 58 y 69 04 66.
FACULTAD DE DERECHO. Paseo al Mar, 24. Telf. 33 27 61, 33 32 20 y 38 40 74.
FACULTAD DE MEDICINA. Paseo al Mar, 17. Telf. 69 04 00 (centralita).
ESCUELA DE INGENIEROS AGRONOMOS Y PERITOS AGRICOLAS. Paseo al Mar.
ESCUELA DE ARQUITECTOS. Palacio Municipal de la Alameda.
ESCUELA DE MAGISTERIO. Alcalde Reig, 1. Telf. 27 79 54.
ESCUELA PROFESIONAL DE COMERCIO. Artes Gráficas, s/n. Telf. 69 15 08.
ESCUELA DE IDIOMAS. En construcción.
ESCUELA SUPERIOR DE BELLAS ARTES. Museo, 2. Telf. 31 26 93.
ESCUELA DE ARTES APLICADAS Y OFICIOS ARTISTICOS. Museo, 8. Telf. 31 05 15 (sucursales: Doctor Gil y Morte, 19. Telf. 26 16 76. Escalante, 9. Telf. 23 12 12).
ESCUELA DE FORMACION PROFESIONAL PESQUERA. Dr. Lluch, 4. Telf. 23 07 96.
ESCUELA DE PERITOS INDUSTRIALES Y ELEMENTAL DEL TRABAJO. José Antonio, 44. Telf. 27 26 00.
INSTITUTO NACIONAL DE ENSEÑANZA MEDIA «LUIS VIVES». Calle de San Pablo. Telf. 21 76 06.
INSTITUTO NACIONAL DE ENSEÑANZA MEDIA «SAN VICENTE FERRER». Calle Almirante Cadarso, 24. Telf. 33 54 77.

ARCHIVOS Y BIBLIOTECAS
ARCHIVES ET BIBLIOTHEQUES
ARCHIVES AND LIBRARIES
ARCHIVE UND BIBLIOTEKEN

ARCHIVO MUNICIPAL. Ayuntamiento.
ARCHIVO DEL PATRIARCA. C. de la Nave.
ARCHIVO DEL REINO. Plaza de Galicia.
BIBLIOTECA ATENEO MERCANTIL. (Para los socios). Plaza del Caudillo.
BIBLIOTECA FACULTAD DE CIENCIAS. Paseo al Mar.
BIBLIOTECA FACULTAD DE DERECHO. Paseo al Mar.
BIBLIOTECA FACULTAD DE FILOSOFIA Y LETRAS. C. Comedias.
BIBLIOTECA MUNICIPAL. Ayuntamiento.
BIBLIOTECA MUNICIPAL. Grao.
BIBLIOTECA POPULAR. Plaza de la Virgen.

ARTESANIA—ARTISANAT
HANDICRAFTS—KUNSTGEWERBE

CIRCULO DE BELLAS ARTES. Plaza de Mariano Benlliure, 6 y 7.
ASOCIACION DE LA PRENSA. Pintor Sorolla, 5.

SALA MATEU. Pintor Sorolla, 15.
SALA PRAT. Correos, 10.
SALA BRAULIO. Pascual y Genís. 3.
GALERIA ESTIL. Isabel la Católica, 23.
GALERIA SAN VICENTE. Lauria, 21.
OFICINA DE INFORMACION Y TURISMO. Paz, 46. (Entrada por la Plaza de Alfonso el Magnánimo).
SALA HOYO. Almirante Cadarso, 4.
MERCADO DE ARTESANIA. Paz, 3.
CERAMICA VALENCIANA. Huerto, 26. Manises.

FERIAS Y FIESTAS

Refiriéndose a Valencia, se ha escrito alguna vez: «Una ciudad que con su trabajo material ha creado riqueza y con su trabajo intelectual ha creado cultura, tiene indudablemente derecho a divertirse. Y desde luego, ejerce ese derecho con toda plenitud». La cosa viene de antiguo, según acreditan autores españoles y extranjeros, en prosa y en verso...

Respecto a las fiestas de pasados tiempos, un ilustre investigador, don Salvador Carreres Zacarés, pudo escribir un libro con casi mil páginas en folio de apretada lectura. Por cierto que dividía las fiestas en ordinarias, las que se celebraban periódicamente, y extraordinarias, las que respondían a un acontecimiento determinado como, por ejemplo, la visita de monarcas, las mutaciones políticas, las victorias bélicas, las beatificaciones y canonizaciones, etc.

En cuanto a las fiestas actuales, también cabe dividirlas, pero aquí bastará citar algunas de las que se celebran a lo largo de cada año.

El 17 de enero, día de San Antonio Abad, se lleva a cabo el primero de los *porrats*, especie de romerías que acontecen en diversas fechas... La Semana Santa alcanza especial brillantez en el distrito Marítimo, con procesiones que tienen como broche un desfile de todas las vistosísimas cofradías, a pleno sol, el domingo de Pascua...

Esta Pascua de Resurrección es aprovechada por los valencianos para salir al campo con objeto de comerse la *mona*, tarta de origen árabe... El lunes de la semana siguiente se celebra la fiesta de San Vicente Ferrer, con los populares *milacres*, representaciones dramáticas en lenguaje vernáculo de milagros efectuados por el Santo, las cuales son ejecutadas por niños en tablados al aire libre... El segundo domingo de mayo se dedica a la Virgen de los Desamparados, con gran alarde de flores... La fiesta del Corpus Christi llegó a soberanos esplendores, compatibles con notas pintorescas...

En cuanto a la Feria de Julio, se celebra poco más o menos en la segunda quincena de dicho mes abunda en corridas de toros y tiene

como final una fastuosa Batalla de Flores...
Aún cabría hablar de otros regocijos públicos;
pero es preferible mencionar el cada vez
más pujante certamen mercantil que es la
Feria Muestrario Internacional, primera im-
plantada en España y que se celebra en el
mes de Mayo.

FOIRES ET FETES

*Se référant à Valence, on a écrit une fois:
«Une ville qui, avec son travail matériel, a
creé de la richesse et avec travail intellectuel,
a creé de la culture, a indiscutablement le
droit de se divertir. En tout cas, elle exerce
ce droit dans toute sa plénitude». La chose
vient de l'antiquité, d'après des auteurs
espagnols et étrangers dignes de fois, en
prose et en vers.*

*En ce qui concerne les fêtes des temps
passés, un illustre chercheur Salvador Carreres Zacarés a puécrire un livre de près
de mille pages de lecture serrée. Il divisait
les fêtes en ordinaires, celles qui sont
célébrées périodiquement, et extraordinaires,
celles qui correspondaient à un événement
déterminé comme, por exemple, la visite de
monarques, les mutations politiques, les
victoires guerrières, les béatifications, cano-
nisations, etc.*

*Quand aux fêtes actuelles, il faut aussi les
diviser mais il suffira d'en citer quelques
unes de celles qui sont célébrées en cours
d'année.*

*Le 17 janvier, jour de St. Antoine Abbé,
a lieu le premier des «Porrats», sorte de
pélerinages qui ont lieu à diverses dates.
La Semaine Sainte atteint une splendeur
spéciale dans le district maritime avec des
processions qui ont comme «clou» un dé-
file de toutes les très spectaculaires con-
fréries en plein soleil, le dimanche de
Pâques.*

*Cette fête de Pâques, les valenciens la
mettent à profit pour aller à la campagne
manger la «mona», tourte d'origine arabe.
Le lundi de la semaine suivante on cé-
lébre la fête de St. Vincent Ferrer, avec
les populaires «milacres», représentations
dramatiques en langage vernaculaire de
miracles accomplis par le Saint, ces représentations etant exécutées par des enfants
sur des estradas en plein air... Le deuxième
dimanche de mai est dédié à la Vierge des
Désemparés avec une grande abondance
de fleurs. La Fête-Dieu atteint une sou-
veraine splendeur compatible avec des
notes pittoresques.*

*Quant à la fête de Juillet, elle a lieu plus ou
moins pendant la deuxième quinzaine de ce
èois. Il y a de nombreuses corridas de taureux
et comme finale une fastueuse bataille de
fleurs.*

Il faudrait encore parler d'autres réjouissan-
ces publiques, mais il est préférable de
mentionner le concours mercantile chaque
fois plus important qu'est la Foire Commer-
ciale Internationale, la première qui fut
implantée en Espagne, et qui a lieu au
mois de Mai.

FAIRS AND FEASTS

Someone has written about Valencia that it
is a «city which has created wealth from
work and has created culture from its intelectual work. It therefore has a right to
enjoi itself, and, fo course, puts that right
into practise in a big way». It is a long
standing tradition, according to both Spanish
and foreing writers of prose and verse...

As far as feasts of the past are concerned,
a famous investigator, Salvador Carreres
Zacarés, was able to write a book of nearly
one thousand pages of closely written
script. He divided the feasts into ordinary
ones, which were the ones held periodically,
and the extraordinary. The latter referred
to special events, such as the visit of
royalty, political changes war victoires,
beatifications and cannonizations, etc.

With regard to current festivities, these
should also be divided, but we shall only
give here some of those held during the
year.

On the 17th January, San Antonio Abad,
the first porrat, a kind of romery, is held,
which are held on different dates... Holy
Week is especially magnificent in the Seafront area, with processions, which end
with a procession of the very showy con-
fraternities, when the sun is at its height,
on Easter Sunday...

Valencians take advantage of Easter Sunday for going out into the country to eat
the «mona», a cake of Arab origin... Easter
Monday is the feast of San Vicente Ferrer,
with the popular «milacres», dramas in
vernacular language on the miracles done
by the Saint. The «milacres» are acted by
children in the open air... The second
sunday in May is dedicated to the Virgin
of the Helples, with agreat gala of flowers...
The feast of Corpus Christi, reaches superb splendours, which are compatible
with picturesque notes...

With regard to the July fair, this is held
more or less in the second fortnight of the
said month. There are many bullfights and
it is closed with a magnificent Battle of
Flowers.

We should still mention other public events:
but it is better to mention the each time
more important event known as the International Samples Fair, the first to be held
in Spain and which is held in May.

JAHRMÄRKTE UND VOLKSFESTE

Man hat einmal über Valencia geschrieben: «Eine Stadt, die mit ihrer körperlichen Arbeit Reichtum und mit ihrer intellektuellen Arbeit Kultur geschaffen hat, hat zweifellos auch das Recht sich zu vergnügen, was sie selbstverständlich auch in vollem Masse tut». Dieses Reacht besitzt Valencia schon seit alters her, wie es spanische und auch ausländische Autoren in ihren Werken bezeugen...

Der Forscher Salvador Carreres Zacarés schrieb ein fast 1.000 Seiten starkes Buch über die Volksfeste vergangener Zeiten. Er teilte sie in gewöhnliche Feste, zu denen die regelmässig wiederkehrenden zählten und in aussergewöhnliche Feste auf, zu denen bestimmte Ereignisse gehörten, so zum Beispiel Monarchenbesuche, Regierung swechsel, Kriegssiege, Selig- und Heiligsprechungen usw.

Auch die heutigen Feste kann man in einzelne Gruppen einteilen, aber wir wollen uns darauf beschränken, hier nur einige der Festlichkeiten, die Jahr für Jahr feierlich begangen werden, aufzuzählen.

Am 17, Jaunar, dem Namensfest des heiligen Antonius, wird die erste der porrats (eine Art Wallfahrt, die an verschiedenen Daten des Jahres stattfindet) veranstaltet. Besonders glanzvoll ist die Karwoche des ans Meer grenzenden Stadtbezirks. Hier kann man Prozessionen bewundern, die am Ostermontag von einem Festzug aller Laienbruderschaften in ihren bunten und prächtigen Trachten abgeschlossen werden...

Am Osterfest pflegen die Valencianer aufs Land zu fahren, um dort ihre mona, eine Torte arabischen Ursprungs, zu essen... Am Montag der folgenden Woche feiert man das Fest zu Ehren von St. Vizenz Ferrer mit den populären milacres. Es sind Schauspiele, die von Kindern unter freiem Himmel in der einheimischen Sprache vorgeführt werden und von den Wundern dieses Heiligen erzählen... Den zweiten Mai-Sonntag widmet man der Virgen de los Desamparados, der an diesem Tage Blumenspenden dargeboten werden... Mit grosser Pracht begeht man das Fronleichnamsfest...

Der Juli-Jahrmarkt findet ungefähr in der zweiten Monatshälfte statt. Er wird von zahlreichen Stierkämpfen begleitet und von einer prunkvollen Blumenschlacht beendet...

Wir müssten noch weitere Volksfeste aufführen, jedoch wollen wir hier nur noch die von Jahr zu Jahr an Bedeutung zunehmende Internationale Mustermesse erwähnen, die als erst in Spanien eingesetzt wurde und im Mai stattfindet.

PLAYAS

PLAYA DE EL PERELLO (SUECA). Playa de arena fina, a 23 km. de la ciudad.
Comunicaciones: Autobuses que salen de la Gran Vía del ·Marqués del Turia, cruce Félix Pizcueta.
CULLERA. A 38 km. de Valencia. Playa de arena fina, dista 2 km. de la población.
Comunicaciones: Línea Férrea Valencia-Cullera, desde la Estación del Norte. Servicio de autobuses desde la Gran Vía de Germanías, 10.
GANDIA. A 66 km. de Valencia. Playa de arena fina situada a 3 km. junto a la desembocadura del río Serpis.
Comunicaciones: Autobuses que parten de la Gran Vía de Germanías, 10.
OLIVA. A 75 km. de Valencia. Playa situada a 4 km. de la ciudad; arena fina.
Comunicaciones: Servicio de autobuses que salen de la Gran Vía de Germanías, 10.

PLAGES

PLAGE DE EL PERELLO (SUECA). Plage de sable fin à 23 km. de la ville.
Communications: autobus qui partent de la Gran Vía del Marqués del Turia, croisement Félix Pizcueta.
CULLERA. A 38 km. de Valence. Plage de sable fin, à 2 km. de la ville.
Communications: voie ferrée Valence-Cullera, de la gare du Nord. Service d'autobus depuis la Gran Vía de Germanías, 10.
GANDIA. A 66 km. de Valence. Plage de sable fin à 3 km. de l'embouchure de la rivière Serpis.
Communications: autobus qui partent de la Gran Vía de Germanías, 10.
OLIVA. A 75 km. de Valence. Plage situé à 4 km. de la ville. Sable fin
Communications: service d'autobus qui partent de la Gran Vía de Germanías, 10.

BEACHES

EL PERELLO BEACH (SUECA). Fine sand beach, 23 kms. from the city
Communications: Bus which leave the Gran Vía del Marqués del Turia, crossroads with Félix Pizcueta
CULLERA. 38 kms. from Valencia. Fine sand beach, 2 kms. from the town.
Communications: Railway line Valencia-Cullera, from North Station. Bus service from Gran Vía de Germanías, 10.
GANDIA. 66 kms. from Valencia. Fine sand beach, 3 kms. away at the mouth of the river Serpis.
Communications: Bus which leave from the Gran Vía de Germanías, 10

OLIVA. 75 kms. from Valencia. Beach 4 kms. away from the town; fine sand.
Communications: Bus service leaving from Gran Vía de Germanías, 10.

STRÄNDE

PLAYA DE EL PERELLO (SUECA). Feiner Sandstrand, 23 Km. von der Stadt entfernt.
Verbindungen: Autobusse fahren von der Gran Vía del Marqués del Turia, Kreuzung Félix Pizcueta ab.
CULLERA. 28 Km. von Valencia entfernt. Feiner Sandstrand, den 2 Km. vom Ort trennen.
Verbindungen: Eisenbahnlinie Valencia-Cullera von der Estación (Bahnhof) dei Norte aus. Autobus-verbindungen von der Gran Vía de Germanías, 10 aus.
GANDIA. 66 Km. von Valencia enfernt. Feiner Sandstrand in der Nähe der Mündung des Serpis, 3 Km. vom Ort entfernt. Verbindungen: Autobusse fahren von der Gran Vía de Germanías, 10 ab.
OLIVA. 15 Km. von Valencia entfernt. Feiner Sandstrand in 4 Km. Entfernung von Oliva. Verbindungen: Autobusse ab Gran Vía de Germanías, 10

GUIAS INTERPRETES Y SUS TARIFAS

GUIDES INTERPRETES ET LEURS TARIFS

INTERPRETER GUIDES AND THEIR CHARGES

FREMDENFÜHRER-DOLMETSCHER UND IHRE TARIFE

BORDANOVE, D. Emilio. C. Sagunto, 5. Telf. 35 03 56. (Ingl. Fr.).
ALTAREJOS, D. Luis Montichelvo, 4. (Fr.).
CALABUIG, Stra. Concha. Obispo Amigo, 3. Telf. 25 33 75 (Fr., Ingl., Alemán).
CLAVER, D. Arturo. Maestro Serrano, 7. Telf. 27 24 66. (Francés).
COSME, D. Francisco. Hotel Royal. Telf. 21 31 21. (Francés, Alemán).
ESQUER, D. Emilio. Bailén, 10. Telf. 22 29 57. (Inglés).
ESQUER. D. Enrique. Bailén, 10. Telf. 22 29 57. Hotel Excelsior. (Francés).
GARCIA, D. José. Angel Guimerá, 28. Telf. 25 76 80. (Francés).
GOMEZ, D. Clemente. Císcar, 46. Telf. 33 06 36. (Francés, Inglés).
JIMENEZ, D. Francisco. Denis, 14. Telf. 27 06 64. (Francés, Inglés).
MARTINEZ, D. Emilio. Hotel Astoria. Telf. 22 77 02. (Inglés).
MARTINEZ, D. Gregorio. Santísimo, 5. Telf. 22 92 44. (Francés).

MATEU, D. Vicente. Goya, 3. Telf. 21 79 14 (Francés).
MORADILLO, D. Gaspar. Salamanca, 29. Telf. 27 48 94. (Inglés).
RAMOS, D. Tomás. Vitoria, 6. Telf. 25 92 50. (Francés).
ROMERO, D. Matías. Paz, 7. Telf. 21 79 14. ((Francés).
SAN MATIAS, D. Francisco. Navas de Tolosa, 2.
TORTOSA, Srta. Amparo. Dr. Sumsi, 28. Telf. 27 88 68. (Francés, Inglés, Italiano)

Tarifas

Medio día: 350 pesetas; Un día: 500 pesetas; Servicios sueltos: 200 pesetas. A partir del 15 de junio.
Por día completo se entiende un período de más de cuatro horas seguidas o con un descanso para almorzar, en cuyo caso la comida es por cuenta del cliente. Medio día menos de 4 horas. Servicios sueltos menos de dos.

Tarifs

Un jour: 500 ptas. Services séparés: 200 ptas. A partir du 15 juin.
Par jour complet on comprend une période de plus de 4 heures d'affilée ou avec un repos pour déjeuner, auquel cas le repas est au compte du client. Demi-jour, moins de 4 heures. Services séparés moins de 2.

Tariffs

Half day: Ptas. 350. One day: Ptas. 500. Loose services: Ptas. 200. As from 15th June.
A complete day is understood to be for a period of more than four hours at a stretch or with a break for lunch, in which case the client shall be for the guide's meal. Half day less than four hours. Loose services less than two hours.

Tarife

Führungen, halbtägig: 350 Peseten; ganztägig: 500 Peseten. Einzelne Führungen: 200 Peseten. Preise gelten am 15 Juni.
Unter ganztägig ist eine ununterbrochene Führung von mehr als 4 Stunden oder aber mit einer Pause zum Mittagessen zu verstehen. In letztem Fall geht das Essen auf Kosten der Besucher. Halbtägige Führungen dauern weniger als 4 und einzelne weniger als 2 Stunden.

ADEMUZ. 3.000 habitantes. A 130 km. de la capital de la provincia. En el centro de la pintoresca comarca llamada Rincón de Ademuz.

ALBAIDA. 4.400 habitantes. A 84 km. Elaboración de cera. Casa-estudio y biblioteca del pintor Segrelles. Fiestas del 5 al 9 de octubre. Es típica la danza de Albaida.

ALBERIQUE. Más de 8.000 habitantes. A 48 km. Su riqueza es proverbial. Elaboración del panquemado.

ALCIRA. Más de 27.000 habitantes. A 37 km. Famosos huertos de naranjos. Producción avícola. Casa Ayuntamiento del siglo XVI. Románicas ruinas del monasterio de la Murta.

ANTELLA. Más de 1.800 habitantes. A 58 km. En pintoresco lugar, nacimiento de la histórica e importante Acequia Real del Júcar.

AYORA. Más de 6.000 habitantes. A 126 km. En el templo arciprestal, valiosas tablas de Yáñez de la Almedina. Histórico castillo.

BENISANO. 1.300 habitantes. A 24 km. Murallas. Palacio-castillo donde estuvo prisionero Francisco I de Francia. En la Iglesia, Virgen del Fundamento, considerada como abogada contra la icterícia.

BETERA. 5.500 habitantes. A 14,35 km. El 15 de agosto, procesión con albahacas de extraordinaria altura.

BICORP. Más de 1.000 habitantes. A 98 km. En su término, la Cueva de la Araña, con importantes pinturas rupestres.

BOCAIRENTE. Más de 3.600 habitantes. A 95 km. Industria textil. Cuadros de Juan de Juanes en la Iglesia parroquial. Curiosas «casetes dels moros» (cuevas abiertas en cantiles).

BUÑOL. Más de 7.000 habitantes. A 40 km. Castillo, donde se alojó Francisco I de Francia. Alrededores muy pintorescos; más de 300 fuentes, cuevas, cascadas.

BURJASOT. Más de 13.000 habitantes. A 4 km. Palacio de San Juan de Ribera, hoy fundación pedagógica. Interesantes silos.

CARCAGENTE. Más de 18.000 habitantes. A 50 km. Famosos huertos de naranjos.

CATARROJA. Más de 11.000 habitantes. A 9 km. En su término embarcadero para La Albufera.

COFRENTES. Unos 1.600 habitantes. A 101 km. En su término, el balneario de los Hervideros. Castillo que domina la confluencia de los ríos Júcar y Cabriel.

CULLERA. Unos 14.000 habitantes. A 40 km. Al pie de una montaña de amplias perspectivas, con santuario de la Virgen. Desembocadura del Júcar. Huertos de mandarinas. Promoción turística.

CHELVA. Unos 3.700 habitantes. A 69 km. Iglesia monumental. Restos de un acueducto romano. Huertas que producen fruta riquísima.

CHULILLA. Unos 1.200 habitantes. A 58 km. Situación pintoresca. Castillo. Imponente desfiladero del río Turia.

ENGUERA. Más de 5.000 habitantes. A 70 km. Tradicional industria textil. En la iglesia parroquial, tabla de la Virgen de Gracia.

GANDIA. Más de 20.000 habitantes. A 70 km.

GILET. Más de 800 habitantes. A 29 km. En su término y en un valle con pinares, el Monasterio franciscano de Sancti Spiritu.

JATIVA. Más de 20.000 habitantes. A 56 km.

LIRIA. Unos 10.000 habitantes. A 25 km. Es la antigua Edeta. Importantes hallazgos ibéricos y romanos. Iglesia de la Sangre (siglo XIV) e iglesia arciprestal (siglo XVII). Palacio de los duques de Alba y Liria. Son magníficas sus dos bandas de música.

MANISES. Unos 13.000 habitantes. A 6 km. Tradicional centro de producción cerámica, que continúa en numerosas fábricas con diversas especialidades.

MOGENTE. Unos 3.000 habitantes. A 76 km. En su término, «La Bastida de les Alcuses» estación prehistórica.

MONCADA. 8.000 habitantes. A 7,6 km. Uno de los numerosos calvarios de la región, con ermita de Santa Bárbara. Semana Santa.

MONTESA. 1.300 habitantes. A 65 km. Ruinas del castillo de la orden militar montesiana, originados por un terremoto en el siglo XVIII.

OLIVA. 13.000 habitantes. A 72 km. Rica ciudad que un tiempo fue rival de la vecina Gandía. Huertos de naranjos.

ONTENIENTE. Unos 19.000 habitantes. A 84 km. Población a un tiempo señorial e industrial. Importante producción de mantas. Setenta industrias textiles con 3.000 obreros.

PATERNA. 17.000 habitantes. A 8 km. Renombrada por su antigua producción cerámica. Torre romana o árabe, según unos u otros autores. Alarde de pólvora en las fiestas al Cristo de la Fe (Agosto).

PUZOL. 6.000 habitantes. A 18 km. En el barrio de «els Hostalets» vio Mérimée a la mujer que le sirvió de modelo físico para su personaje «Carmen». En el monte Picayo, hotel con piscina.

REQUENA. 21.000 habitantes. A 76 km. Portadas góticas de Santa María y del Salvador. Casona llamada palacio del Cid. Barrio antiguo. Estación de Enología. Museo del vino.

PUIG, El. 3.000 habitantes. A 15 km. Lugar donde partió la reconquista de Valencia por Jaime I. Gran monasterio mercedario. Recuerdos históricos.

SAGUNTO. Unos 41.000 habitantes, entre la ciudad y el barrio del puerto, formado junto a la factoría siderúrgica. A 25 km.

SERRA. Unos 1.500 habitantes. A 26,5 km. Castillo. Término accidentado y pintoresco. Lugar de veraneo. A 6 km. de la población, en un valle delicioso, la histórica cartuja de Porta-Coeli.

SUECA. Más de 20.000 habitantes. A 34 km. Gran centro de producción arrocera. El Perelló, a 10 km., en la costa, es lugar de veraneo.

TORRENTE. Más de 16.000 habitantes. A 9 km. A los pies del monte El Vedat, zona de veraneo, con pinar, desde la que se domina parte de la Huerta con Valencia al fondo.

VILLAR DEL ARZOBISPO. Más de 4.000 habitantes. A 49 km. Conserva mucho tipismo, en sus calles y plazas y hasta en sus costumbres. Goza nombradía de muy saludable.

EXCURSIONS DE VALENCE A LA PROVINCE

ADEMUZ. 3.000 hab. A 130 km. de la capitale de la province. Au centre de la pittoresque région appelée Rincón de Ademuz.

ALBAIDA. 4.400 hab. A 84 km. Elaboration de cire. Maison-studio et bibliothèque du fameux peintre Segrelles. Fêtes du 5 au 9 octobre. La danse de Albaida est typique.

ALBERIQUE. Plus de 8.000 hab. A 48 km. Sa richesse est proverbiale. Elaboration du «panquemado».

ALCIRA. Plus de 27.000 hab. A 37 km. Fameuses plantations d'orangers. Production avicole. Hôtel de Ville du XVIᵉ s. Ruines roman du monastère de la Murta.

ANTELLA. Plus de 1.800 hab. A 58 km. Dans un endroit pittoresque, naissance de l'historique et important Canal Royal du Júcar.

AYORA. Plus de 6.000 hab. A 126 km. Dans le temple de l'archiprêtre, précieuses planche de Yáñez de la Almedina. Château historique.

BENISANO. 1.300 hab. A 24 km. —Murailles— palais-château fort où fut prisonnier François I de France. Dans l'église, Vierge «del Fundamento», considérée comme avocate contre la jaunisse.

BETERA. 5.500 hab. A 14,35 km. Le 15 août, procession avec des «albahacas» (basilic) d'une extraordinaire hauteur.

BICORP. Plus de 1.000 hab. A 98 km. Sur son territoire, la Cueva de la Araña avec d'importantes peintures rupestres.

BOCAIRENTE. Plus de 3.600 hab. A 95 km. Industrie textile. Tableaux de Juan de Juanes dans l'église paroissiale. Curieuses «casetes dels moros» (cavernes ouvertes sur des falaises).

BUÑOL. Plus de 7.000 hab. A 40 km. Château où logea François I de France. Environs très pittoresques. Plus de 300 sources, cavernes, cascades.

BURJASOT. Plus de 13.000 hab. A 4 km. Palais de St. Jean de la Ribera, aujourd'hui fondation pédagogique. Silos intéressants.

CARCAGENTE. Plus de 18.000 hab. A 50 km. Fameuses plantations d'orangers.

CATARROJA. Plus de 11.000 hab. A 9 km. L'embarcadère pour La Albufera se trouve sur son territoire.

COFRENTES. Environ 1.600 hab. A 101 km. Sur son territoire, la station balnéaire de Los Hervideros. Château qui domine la confluence des rivières Júcar et Cabriel.

CULLERA. Environ 14.000 hab. A 40 km. Au pied d'une montagne de vastes perspectives, avec un sanctuaire de la Vierge. Embouchure du Júcar. Plantations de mandarines. Promotion touristique.

CHELVA. Environ 3.700 hab. A 69 km. Eglise monumentale. Restes d'un aqueduc romain. Huertas qui produisent des fruits tres savoureux.

CHULILLA. Environ 1.200 hab. A 58 km. Situation pittoresque. Château. Imposant défilé du Turia.

ENGUERA. Plus de 5.000 hab. A 70 km. Industrie textile traditionnelle. Dans l'église paroissiale, planche de la Vierge de Grâce.

GANDIA. Plus de 20.000 hab. A 70 km.

GILET. Plus de 800 hab. A 29 km. Sur son territoire, il y a dans une vallée avec des pins le monastère franciscain de Sancti Spiritu.

JATIVA. Plus de 20.000 hab. A 56 km.

LIRIA. Environ 10.000 hab. A 25 km. C'est l'ancienne Edeta. Importantes trouvailles ibériques et romaines. Eglise du Sang (XIVᵉ) et église de l'archiprêtre (XVIIᵉ). Palais des Ducs d'Albe et Liria. Deux magnifiques fanfares.

MANISES. Environ 13.000 hab. A 6 km. Centre traditionnel de production céramique, qui continue dans les nombreuses fabriques, avec diverses spécialités.

MOGENTE. Environ 3.000 hab. A 76 km. Sur son territoire «La Bastida de les Alcuses», station préhistorique.

MONCADA. 8.000 hab. A 7,6 km. Un des nombreux calvaires de la région, avec ermitage de Ste. Barbe. Semaine Sante.

MONTESA. 1.300 hab. A 65 km. Ruines du Château de l'ordre militaire montésien, causées par un tremblement de terre au XVIIIᵉ.

OLIVA. 13.000 hab. A 72 km. Riche cité qui fut pendant un temps rivale de la voisine Gandia. Plantations d'orangers.

ONTENIENTE. Environ 19.000 hab. A 84 km. Agglomération à la fois seigneuriale et industrielle. Importante production de couvertures. Soixante dix industries extiles avec 3.000 ouvries.

PATERNA. 17.000 hab. A 8 km. Renommée pour son ancienne production céramique. Tour romaine ou arabe selon les uns ou les autres auteurs. Débauche de poudre pendant les fêtes du Christ de la Foi (août).

PUZOL. 6.000 hab. A 18 km. Dans le quartier de «els Hostalets» Mérimée vit la femme qui servit de modèle physique pour son personnage «Carmen», Au Mont Picayo, hôtel avec piscine.

REQUENA. 21.000 hab. A 76 km. Portiques gothiques de Santa María et del Salvador. Maison appelée palais du Cid. Quartier ancien. Station d'Oenologie. Musée du vin.

PUIG (EL). 3.000 hab. A 15 km. Endroit d'où partit la reconquête de Valence por Jaime I Grand monastère de la Merced. Souvenirs historiques.

SAGUNTO. Environ 41.000 hab. Entre la ville et le quartier du port le quartier du port formé à côté de la fabrique sidérurgique. A 25 km.

SERRA. Environ 1.500 hab. A 26,5 km. Château. Territoire accidenté et pittoresque. Endroit de villégiature. A 6 km de l'agglomération, dans une delicieuse vallée, l'historique chartreuse de Porta-Coeli.

SUECA. Plus de 20.000 hab. A 34 km. Grand centre de production de riz. El Perelló, à 10 km. sur la côté, est un lieu de villégiature.

TORRENTE. Plus de 16.000 hab. A 9 km. Au pieds du mont El Vedat zone de villégiature d'où l'on domine une partie de la Huerta avec Valence au fond.

VILLAR DEL ARZOBISPO. Plus de 4.000 hab. A 49 km. Conserve beaucoup de typisme dans ses rues, ses places et même ses coutumes. A la réputation d'être très salubre.

EXCURSIONS FROM VALENCIA TO THE PROVINCE

ADEMUZ. 3.000 inhabitants. 130 kms. From the capital of the province. In the centre of picturesque region called Rincón de Ademuz.

ALBAIDA. 4.400 inhabitants. 84 kms. Manufacture of wax. House-studio and library of the painter Segrelles. Festivites from 5th to 9th October. The dance of Albaida is typical.

ALBERIQUE. More than 8.000 inhabitants. 48 kms. away. Its wealth is proverbial. Manufacture of the «panquemado».

ALCIRA. More than 27.000 inhabitants. 37 kms. Famous orange orchards. Chicken farms. 16th century Town Hall. Romanesque ruins of the monastery of La Murta.

ANTELLA. More than 1.800 inhabitants. 58 kms. In a picturesque sport, the birthplace of the historic and important Acequia Real del Júcar.

AYORA. More than 6.000 inhabitants. 126 kms. In the archpriest chuch, valuable, plaque by Yáñez de la Almedina. Historic castle.

BENISANO. 1.300 inhabitants. 24 kms. Walls. Palace-Castle where Francis I of France was held prisoner. In the church of Virgin del Fundamento, considered as the defender against jaundice.

BETERA. 5.500 inhabitants. 14,35 kms. On 15th August, procession with extraordinarily high basil plants.

BICORP. More than 1.000 inhabitants. 98 kms. Within its boundaries, the Cueva de la Araña, with important Rupestrian paintings.

BOCAIRENTE. More than 3.600 inhabitants. 95 kms. Textile industry. Pictures by Juan de Juanes in the parish church. Curious «casetes dels moros» (open caves in cliff).

BUÑOL. More than 7.000 inhabitants. 40 kms. Castle where Francis I of France stayed. Very picturesque surrounds: more than 300 fountains, caves, waterfalls.

BURIASOT. More than 13.000 inhabitants. 4 kms. Palace of San Juan de Ribera, today a pedagogic foundation. Interesting silos.

CARCAGENTE. More than 18.000 inhabitants. 50 kms. Famous orange groves.

CATARROJA. More than 11.000 inhabitants. 9 kms. In its boundaries pier for the Albufera.

COFRENTES. Some 1.600 inhabitants. 101 kms. Within its boundaries; the Hervideros Spa. Castle which dominantes the confluence of the rivers Júcar and Cabriel.

CULLERA. Some 14.000 inhabitants. 40 kms. at the foot of a mountain with wide views, and sanctuary to the Virgin. Mouth of the Júcar. Mandarin groves. Tourist promotion centre.

CHELVA. Some 3.700 inhabitants. 69 kms. Monumental church. Remains of a roman aqueduct. Orchards which produce delicious fruit.

CHULILLA. Some 1.200 inhabitants. 58 kms. Picturesque situation. Castle. Important pass of the river Turia.

ENGUERA. More than 5.000 inhabitants. 70 kms. Traditional Textile industry. In the parish church plaque of the Virgin de Gracia.

GANDIA. More than 22.000 inhabitants. 70 kms.

GILET. More than 800 inhabitants. 29 kms. Within its boundaries and in an pine tree valley. the Franciscan monastery of the Sancti Spíritu.

JATIVA. More than 20.000 inhabitants. 56 kms.

LIRIA. Some 10.000 inhabitants. 25 kms. This is the former Edeta. Important Iberian and Roman findings Church of the Sangre (14th century) and archpriest church (17th century). Palace of the Dukes of Alba and Liria. The two music bands are magnificent.

MANISES. Some 13.000 inhabitants. 6 kms. Traditional centre of ceramic manufacture, with numerous factories specializing in different things.

MOGENTE. Some 3.000 inhabitants. 76 kms. Within its boundaries «La Bastida de les Alcuses» prehistoric settlement.

MONCADA. 8.000 inhabitants. 7,6 kms. One of the numerous calvaries of the region, with hermitage of Santa Bárbara. Holy Week.

MONTESA. 1.300 inhabitants. 65 kms. Ruins

of the castle of the Montesian military order producer by an earthquake in the 18th century.

OLIVA. 13.000 inhabitants. 72 kms. A rich town which was at one time a rival of Gandía its neighbour. Orange groves.

ONTENIENTE. Some 19.000 inhabitants. 84 kms. Aristocratic as well as industrial town Important production of blankets. Seventy textile industries with 3.000 workmen.

PATERNA. 17.000 inhabitants. 8 kms. Renowned for its former cermics production. Roman or Arab tower, according to some authors and others. Fireworks during the fiestas of Cristo de la Fe (August).

PUZOL. 6.000 inhabitants. 18 kms. In the district of «els Hostalets». Mérimée saw the woman who was his physical model for his character «Carmen». On the monte Picayo, hotel with swimming pool.

REQUENA. 21.000 inhabitants. 76 kms. Gothic porches of Santa María and El Salvador. Mansion called El Cid's palace. Old district. Wine investigation centre. Wine Museum.

PUIG (EL). 3.000 inhabitants. 15 kms. Place where the conquest of Valencia by Jaime I began. Great Mercedarian monastery. Historical remains.

SAGUNTO. 41.000 inhabitants. Befween the city and the port quarter. 25 kms. away.

SERRA. Some 1.500 inhabitants. 26,5 kms. Castle. Mountainous and picturesque area. Summer resort. 6 kms. from the twon, the historical Carthusain monastery of Porta-Coeli in a delightful valley.

SUECA. More than 20.000 inhabitants. 34 kms. Great rice producing centre. El Perelló, 10 kms. away, on the coast, is a summer resort.

TORRENTE. More than 16.000 inhabitants. 9 kms. away. At the foot cf the El Vedat mountain, from which one can see the Valencian orchard with the city in the background.

VILLAR DEL ARZOBISPO. More than 4.000 inhabitants. 49 kms. away. Very typical, especially with regard to the streets and square and even in the customs. It is said to be very healthy.

EXKURSIONEN VON VALENCIA IN DIE PROVINZ

ADEMUZ. 3.000 Einwohner. 130 km. von der Hauptstadt entfernt. Liegt im Zentrum des malerischen Landstrichs Rincón de Ademuz.

ALBAIDA. 4.400 Einwohner. 84 km. von Valencia entfernt. Wachs-Herstellung. Haus mit Studium sowie Bibliothek des Malers Segrelles. Volksfest 5. - 9. Oktober. Typisch ist der Volkstanz von Albaida.

ALBERIQUE. Über 8.000 Einwohner. 48 km von Valencia entfernt. Sein Reichtum ist sprichwörtlich. Herstellung von «panquemado».

ALCIRA. Über 27.000 Einwohner. 37 km. von Valencia entfernt. Berühmte Apfelsinenplantagen. Geflügelfarmen. Rathaus aus dem XVI. Jahrh. Romanisch. Ruinen des Klosters de la Murta.

ANTELLA. Über 1.800 Einwohner. 58 km. von Valencia entfernt. Liegt in einer malerischen Landschaft, in der der historische und bedeutende Acequia (Bewässerungskanal) Real del Júcar entstand.

AYORA. Über 6.000 Einwohner. 126 km. von Valencia entfernt. In der Erzpriesterkirche befinden sich wartvolle Gemälde auf Holz von Yáñez de la Almedina. Historische Burg.

BENISANO. 1.300 Einwohner. 24 km. von Valencia entfernt. Stadtmauern. Burgpalast, in dem Franz I. von Frankreich gefangengehalten wurde. In der Kirche Madonnenstatue der Virgen del Fundamento, die als Schutzpatronin der Gelbsüchtigen verehrt wird.

BETERA. 5.500 Einwohner. 14,35 km. von Valencia entfernt. Am 15. August findem Prozessionen mit aussergewöhnlich grossen albahacas (wohlriechende Blumenart) statt.

BICORP. Über 1.000 Einwohner. 98 km. von Valencia entfernt. Im Bezirk dieses Ortes befindet sich die Cueva de la Araña (Spinnen Höhle) mit bedeutenden Felsmalereien.

BOCAIRENTE. Über 3.600 Einwohner. 95 km. von Valencia entfernt. Textil-Industrie. Gemälde von Juan de Juanes in der Pfarrkirche. Sehenswerte «casetes del moro» (offene Höhlen in steilen Klippen).

BUÑOL. Über 7.000 Einwohner. 40 km. von Valencia entfernt. Burg, im der Franz I. von Frankreich wohnte. Malerische Umgebung; Über 300 Quellen, Höhlen, Wasserfälle.

BURJASOT. Über 13.000 Einwohner. 4 km. von Valencia entfernt. Palast von San Juan de Ribera, heute pädagogische Stiftung. Interessante Silos.

CARCAGENTE. Über 18.000 Einwohner. 50 km. von Valencia entfernt. Berühmte Apfelsinenplantagen.

CATARROJA. Über 11.000 Einwohner. 9 km. von Valencia entfernt. In seinem Bezirk Anlegeplatz der Schiffe nach La Albufera.

COFRENTES. Ungefähr 1.600 Einwohner. 101 km. von Valencia entfernt. In seinem Bezirk Balneario (Kurhaus) de los Hervidores. Burg am Zusammenfluss des Júcar und Cabriel.

CULLERA. Ungefähr 14.000 Einwohner. 40 km. von Valencia entfernt. Am Fusse eines Berges, der eine schöne Aussicht gestattet und auf dem sich das Sanktuarium der Jungfrau María befindet. Mündung des Júcar. Mandarinenplantagen. Touristenort.

CHELVA. Ungefähr 3.700 Einwohner. 69 km. von Valencia entfernt. Monumentale Kirche. Überreste einer römischen Wasserleitung. Reiche Obstplantagen.

CHULILLA. Ungefähr 1.200 Einwohner. 58 km. von Valencia entfernt. Malerischer Ort.

Burg. Grossartiger Engpass des Flusses Turia.

ENGUERA. Über 5.000 Einwohner. 70 km. von Valencia entfernt. Traditionelle Textilindustrie. In der Pfarrkirche Gemälde auf Holz der Virgen de Gracia.

GANDIA. Über 20.000 Einwohner. 70 km. von Valencia entfernt.

GILET. Über 800 Einwohner. 29 km. von Valencia entfernt. In der Umgebung in einem mit Kiefern bewachsenen. Tal Franziskanerkloster Sancti Spiritu.

JATIVA. Über 20.000 Einwohner. 56 km. von Valencia entfernt.

LIRIA. Ungefähr 10.000 Einwohner. 25 km. von Valencia entfernt. Es ist das antike Edeta. Bedeutende iberische und römische Funde. Kirche de la Sangre (XIV. Jahrh.) und Erzpriesterkirche (XVII. Jahrh.). Palast der Herzöge von Alba und Liria. Nennenswert sind seine zwei Musikkapellen.

MANISES. Ungefähr 13.000 Einwohner. 6 km. von Valencia entfernt. Zentrum traditioneller Keramik-Herstellung, die in zahlreichen Fabriken fortgesetzt wird.

MOGENTE. Ungefähr 3.000 Einwohner. 76 km. von Valencia entfernt. In seinem Bezirk befindet sich «La Bastida de les Alcuses», ein prähistorischer Ort.

MONCADA. 8.000 Einwohner. 7,6 km. von Valencia entfernt. Einer der zahlreichen Kalvarienberge dieser Region mit Wallfahrtskapelle Santa Bárbara. Karwoche.

MONTESA. 1.300 Einwohner. 65 km. von Valencia entfernt. Ruinen der Burg des Montesa-Ordens, die infolge eines Erdbebens im XVIII. Jahrh. entstanden.

OLIVA. 13.000 Einwohner. 72 km. von Valencia entfernt. Reiche Stadt, die eine Zeitlang Revalin des benachbarten Gandia war. Apfelsinenplantagen.

ONTENIENTE. Ungefähr 19.000 Einwohner. 84 km. von Valencia entfernt. Ein herrschaftlicher und zugleich industrieller Ort. Bedeutende Decken-Fabrikation. 70 Textilbetriebe mit 3.000 Arbeitern.

PATERNA. 17.000 Einwohner. 8 km. von Valencia entfernt. Berühmt wegen seiner alten Keramik-Herstellung. Römischer oder nach Meinung anderer Forscher arabischer Turm. Fest des Cristo de la Fe (August) mit Feuerwerk.

PUZOL. 6.000 Einwohner. 18 km. con Valencia entfernt. Im Stadtviertel «els Hostalets» sah Mérimée das Modell für die Darstellung seiner «Carmen». Auf dem Berg Picayo Hotel mit Schwimmbecken.

REQUENA. 21.000 Einwohner. 76 km. von Valencia entfernt. Gotische Portale von Santa Maria und el Salvador. Prächtiges Haus, genannt Palast des Cid. Altes Stadtviertel. Weinanbau. Wein-Museum.

PUIG, EL. 3.000 Einwohner. 15 km. von Valencia entfernt. Von diesem Ort aus brach Jaime I. zur Wiedereroberung Va-

lencias auf. Grosses Kloster der barmherzigen Brüder. Historische Andenken.

SAGUNTO. Zahl der Einwohner ungefähr 41.000, die sich aus den Bewohnern der Stadt und des Hafenstadtteils zusammensetzt. 25 km. von Valencia entfernt.

SERRA. Ungefähr 1.500 Einwohner. 26,5 km. von Valencia entfernt. Burg. Hügelige und malerische Umgebung. Sommererholungssort. 6 km. von Ort entfernt befindet sich in einem herrlichen Tal das historische Kartäuserkloster Porta-Coeli.

SUECA. Über 20.000 Einwohner. 34 km. von Valencia entfernt. Grosse und zahlreiche Reisfelder. El Perelló, ungefähr 10 km. von Sueca entfernt, liegt an der Küste und ist Sommererholungsort.

TORRENTE. Über 16.000 Einwohner. 9 km. von Valencia entfernt. Am Fusse des Berges El Vedat befindet sich ein Feriengebiet mit Fichtenwald, das einen Blick a uf die Huerta mit Valencia im Hintergrund gestattet.

VILLAR DEL ARZOBISPO. Über 4.000 Einwohner. 49 km. von Valencia entfernt. Hat in seinen Strassen und plätzen und sogar seinen Bräuchen seinen eigenen Charakter bewahrt. Das Klima dieses Ortes wird für sehr heilsam gehalten.

BALNEARIOS DE LA PROVINCIA

BELLUS. Reuma y nervios. Informes: Admor. Balneario. Temporada: 20-6 al 20-10.

CHULILLA. Digestivo, nutrición y piel. Informes: D. Emilio Cervera. Bisbesa, 5. Valencia. Temporada: 1-6 al 15-9.

FUENTE PODRIDA (Requena). Digestivo y nutrición. Informes: Admor. Balneraio. Temporada: 15-16 al 30-5.

HERVIDEROS (Cofrentes). Digestivo y nutrición. Informes: Marqués de Dos Aguas, 5. Valencia. Temporada: 1-7 al 20-10.

MOLINELL (Oliva). Digestivo, nutrición, piel y reuma. Informes: Mártires, 27. Piles (Valencia). Temporada: 20-6 al 20-10.

SANTA ANA (Llosa de Ranes). Digestivo, nutrición, piel y reuma. Informes: Sagasta, 6. Valencia. Temporada: 1-6 al 3-9.

SANTO TOMAS. Sto. Tomás. Valencia. Digestivo y piel. Informes: Da. Concepción Lafuente. Serrano, 22. Puerto. Temporada: 1-6 al 31-10.

STATIONS BALNEAIRES DE LA PROVINCE

BELLUS. Rhumatisme et nerfs. Informations: Admor, Balneario, Saison 20-6 au 20-10.

CHULILLA. Digestion, nutrition et peau. Informations. D. Emilio Cervera. Bisbesa, 5. Valence. Saison, 1-6 au 15-9.

FUENTE PODRIDA (Requena). Digestion et

nutrition. Informations: Admor. Balneario. Saison 15-16 au 30-5.

HERVIDEROS (Cofrentes). Digestion et nutrition. Informations: Marqués de Dos Aguas, 5. Valence. Saison 1-7 au 20-10.

MOLINELL (Oliva). Digestion, nutrition, peau et rhumatisme, Inform. Mártires, 27. Piles (Valence). Saison 20-6 au 20-10.

SANTA ANA (Llosa de Ranes). Digestion, nutrition, peau et rhumatisme. Sagasta, 6. Valence. Saison: 1-6 au 3-9.

SANTO TOMAS. Sto. Tomás. Valence. Digestion et peau. Inform. Da Conception Lafuente. Serrano, 22. Puerto. Saison: 1-6 au 31-10.

SPAS IN THE PROVINCE

BELLUS. Rheumatism and nerves. Information: Admor. Balneario. Season 20-6 to 20-10.

CHULILLA. Digestive, nutrition and skin. Information: D. Emilio Cervera. Bisbesa, 5. Valencia. Season 1-6 to 15-9.

FUENTE PODRIDA (Requena). Digestive and nutrition. Information: Admor. Balneario. Season 15-6 to 30-5.

HERVIDEROS (Cofrentes). Digestive and nutrition. Information: Marqués de Dos Aguas, 5. Valencia. Season: 1-7 to 20-10.

MOLINELL (Oliva). Digestive, nutrition, skin and rheumatism. Information: Mártires, 27. Piles (Valencia). Season 20-6 to 20-10.

SANTA ANA (Llosa de Ranes). Digestive, nutrition, skin and rheumatism. Information: Sagasta, 6. Valencia. Season 1-6 to 3-9.

SANTO TOMAS. Sto. Tomás. Valencia. Digestive and skin. Information: Mrs. Concepción Lafuente. Serrano, 22. Port. Season: 1-6 to 31-10.

KUR- UND BADEORTE DER GANZEN PROVINZ

BELLUS. Rheumatismus und Nervenkrankheiten. Auskunft: Geschäftsführer des Kurhauses. Saison: 20.6 - 20.10.

CHULILLA. Krankheiten des Verdauungsapparates, Ernährungs- und Hautkrankheiten. Auskunft: Emilio Cervera. Valencia, Bisbesa, 5. Saison: 1.6 - 15.9.

FUENTE PODRIDA (Requena). Krankheiten des Verdauungsapparates und Ernährungskrankheiten. Auskunft: Geschäftsführer des Kurhauses. Saison: 15.6. - 30.5.

HERVIDEROS (Cofrentes). Krankheiten des Verdauungsapparates und Ernährungskrankheiten. Auskunft: Valencia, Marqués de Dos Aguas 5. Saison: 1.7. - 20.10.

MOLINELL (Oliva). Verdauungs-, Ernährungs- und Hautkrankheiten, Rheumatismus. Auskunft: Piles (Valencia), Mártires 27. Saison: 20.6. - 20.10.

SANTA ANA (Llosa de Ranes). Verdauungs-, Ernährungs- und Hautkrankheiten, Rheumatismus. Auskunft: Valencia, Sagasta 6. Saison: 1.6. - 3.9.

SANTO TOMAS. Santo Tomás. Valencia. Krankheiten des Verdauungsapparates und Hautkrankheiten. Auskunft: Doña Concepción Lafuente. Serrano 22. Puerto (Hafen). Saison: 1.6. - 31.10.

DISTANCIAS KILOMETRICAS DESDE VALENCIA A:

DISTANCES KILOMETRIQUES DE VALENCIA A:

DISTANCES IN KILOMETERS FROM VALENCIA TO:

ENTFERNUNGEN IN KM. VON VALENCIA NACH:

Albacete	171
Alicante	166
Barcelona	352
Castellón	64
Cuenca	223
Madrid	350
Murcia	242
Teruel	145

RUTA HISTORICA DE SAGUNTO
RUTA HISTORICA DE LIRIA
RUTA DEL VINO
RUTA DEL ARROZ
RUTA DEL NARANJO
RUTA DE JATIVA – AYORA – COFRENTES

✗ CAZA
▲ CAMPING
ALBERGUE, PARADOR, REFUGIO
HOSTERIA DE LA D.G.T.
MONUMENTOS
RECURSOS TURISTICOS
PESCA
DEPORTES NAUTICOS
PLAYA